COLOURS OF THE INDUS

Costume and Textiles of Pakistan

This book has been published to coincide with the exhibition 'Colours of the Indus: Costume and Textiles of Pakistan', first shown at the Victoria and Albert Museum, London, 9 October 1997 – 29 March 1998, in commemoration of the fiftieth anniversary of Pakistan.

Half-title page: Kalash girl in a group dance, Birir Valley, Chitral, 1996
Frontispiece: Meghwar woman wearing festive clothes: a block-printed yellow cotton skirt (parha), an embroidered blouse front (gaj) and a red cotton tie-dyed headshawl (bandhani); Bhalwa village, Chachro, Tharparkar, 1994
Front jacket/cover: Detail of a waist-cloth (lungi or lacha), fig. 142, p. 91
Back jacket/cover: Faqirani Jat women returning home from a pilgrimage at Shah Bandar, Thatta, Indus delta, 1996

First published 1997, in association with the Victoria and Albert Museum, by
Merrell Holberton Publishers Ltd
Willcox House, 42 Southwark Street, London SE1 1UN

Text © Nasreen Askari and the Board of Trustees of the Victoria and Albert Museum
Photographs © the Board of Trustees of the Victoria and Albert Museum except as credited on p. 144

Produced by Merrell Holberton Publishers
Designed by Roger Davies
Printed in Italy

Contents

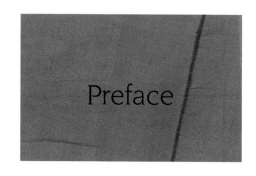

Preface

On its fiftieth anniversary, Pakistan remains an enigma. The seat of one of the world's oldest civilizations, it covers the entire western aspect of the South Asian subcontinent, but springs into view only because of its volatile politics, its competitive sportsmen and the occasional socialite. The artistic traditions to which it is heir have generally been subsumed into the fields of Indian art and culture without much debate or discussion. This book and its accompanying exhibition at the Victoria and Albert Museum celebrate the validity and distinctiveness of the artistic traditions of Pakistan.

Nowhere is this tradition more apparent than in the enormous diversity of its textiles. Pakistan's geographical position has made it a crucible in which influences from Europe, Turkey, Iran, Afghanistan, Central Asia and China have fused with the indigenous traditions of South Asia. Buddhism, Hinduism, Zoroastrianism and Islam have also intermingled here to add to the legacy of ritual and pattern. Each of the regional textile traditions of Pakistan, the Pathan, the Punjabi, the Baluch and that of Sindh, has evolved a range of design, form and technique that is a distillation not only of local traditions, but, over time, from those further afield.

Colours of the Indus is a pioneering event as it marks the first ever exposition of Pakistan's rich but little known costumes and textiles. It has drawn on the large collections of the Victoria and Albert Museum, and on museums and private collections throughout Pakistan, in Japan and the United Kingdom. We are greatly indebted to all those individuals who have so generously permitted us to borrow objects from their personal collections and we have been sustained by the faith that they have had in our endeavour. If we succeed, in some small measure, in demonstrating the relevance of the textile traditions of Pakistan to the wider region of South Asia, this effort will have been more than worth while.

NASREEN ASKARI AND ROSEMARY CRILL

Acknowledgements

Colours of the Indus would not have been possible without the enthusiasm and support of many who gave of their time and counsel but have chosen to remain anonymous. We would like in particular to express our deep appreciation to a number of institutions and individuals whose financial support has been critical in making the exhibition possible: the Government of Sindh, Pakistan; ABN Amro Bank; The Bestway Foundation, London; Mrs Shehrbano Hassam Ismail and family, Karachi; The Pak-Arab Refinery Company, Karachi; The Barakat Trust, Oxford; The Ondaatje Foundation, Toronto; and Visiting Arts, London.

Colours of the Indus owes an immeasurable debt of gratitude to Abdul Hamid Akhund, who has been involved in every aspect of its organization, from fund-raising, the diligent planning of field trips across Pakistan, obtaining potential loans and inspiring field photography to unfailingly giving information and time. Among those who opened their homes and offered unstinting hospitality, Mr and Mrs Huzoor Buksh Dombki, Mr and Mrs Hur Riahi Gardezi, Mrs Abida Hussain, Mr and Mrs Zulfiqar Ali Shah Jamote, Mrs Parveen Magsi, Sardar and Begum Sherbaz Mazari, Makhdoom Sajjad Hussain Qureshi, Mrs Fauzia Khawar Ali Shah and Mr and Mrs Ahmed Nawaz Shinwari deserve our special thanks. Nawab Akbar Khan Bugti magnanimously arranged for us to stay in Dera Bugti and allowed us valuable insights, through personal reminiscences, into the cultural history of Baluchistan.

Owners of private collections were extremely generous both in allowing us access to their collections and providing information, and in many cases lending pieces for the exhibition. In this connection we are very grateful to Professor Anita Ghulamali, Faqir Aijazuddin, Rani Atiqa Ghazanfar of Hunza, Nawab Akbar Khan Bugti, Fauzia Khawar Ali Shah, Sehyr Saigol, Banto Kazmi and Faiza Samee in Pakistan, together with Pip Rau, John Gillow, Sheila Paine, Venice and Alastair Lamb and Steven Cohen in England. We would like to thank Hiroko Iwatate in Tokyo for sending information on pieces in her collection, several of which she has lent us for the exhibition. We are also grateful to Dr S.R. Dar of the Lahore Museum, Uxi Mufti, Dr S.M. Zaidi and Khalid Javaid of the Lok Virsa, Islamabad, Dr Parveen Nasir of the National Museum of Pakistan, Karachi, Dr Brian Durrans and Imogen Laing of the Dept of Ethnography, The British Museum, and Dr Schuyler Jones and Graham Coote of the Pitt Rivers Museum, Oxford, for permitting us to see collections in their care.

Ghaffar Mohmand and Hayat Ali Shah of the Sarhad Tourism Development Corporation of Pakistan arranged our travel to remote villages and settlements in the valleys of the North-West Frontier from Indus Kohistan across Swat and into Chitral. Members of the Directorate of Culture, Sindh, including Syed Zafar Kazmi, Rabia Jamil Zubedi, Ayub Jamali and the late Mumtaz Mirza provided ideas and background. Mohammed Ali Qadri conscientiously carried out field photography, while Professor A.H. Dani, Dr Nabi Buksh Baloch, Dr Harchandrai, Jagdish Magaram, Mohammed Hussain Kashif and Mohammed Ramzan Jat all gave us good advice.

Within the Victoria and Albert Museum, many people have contributed to the exhibition. We would like to acknowledge the special support of Dr Deborah Swallow, Chief Curator of the Indian and South-East Asian Department, Lynda Hillyer, and the Textiles Conservation Department. We are grateful to Mike Kitcatt of the Photographic Studio for taking the majority of the studio photographs and to Divia Patel of the Indian and South-East Asian Department for assisting with the photography. Finally, a particular mention of Noelle Hurrell for her cheerful secretarial assistance.

A Brief History of Textiles in Pakistan

Although Pakistan is only fifty years old as an independent country, it is the site of the earliest evidence of settled society in South Asia. The Indus Valley and Harappan sites, dating from the fourth millennium BC, are now well known, but much earlier even than these is the large settlement where excavations began in 1974 at Mehrgarh in Baluchistan, which dates back to the seventh millennium BC. A sophisticated material culture was certainly in place there by about 5000 BC, and a wealth of decorated pottery from that period has been excavated. Most significant for our purpose, however, is an impression of a woven fabric found in one of the grave sites,[1] together with large finds of cotton seed datable to the fifth millennium BC.[2] These represent the earliest evidence both of cotton cultivation and of textile-weaving in the subcontinent.[3] No physical examples survive from this early period: it is in the organic nature of textiles to decompose in the earth, so evidence of prehistoric weaving technology tends to be indirect, whether by the impression of woven patterns in the medium of burial, as at Mehrgarh, or by the presence of textile-related tools such as needles or spindle-whorls, both of which have been found at Mohenjodaro, the Indus Valley site datable to about 2500 BC. Mohenjodaro has also provided us with the earliest actual textile sample from the subcontinent: cotton threads dyed apparently with madder, a crucial piece of evidence that the craftsmen of the Indus Valley were familiar with cotton processing and dyeing technology centuries before other cultures.[4] A striking depiction of a patterned cloth from this period is seen in the stone statue of a bearded man, possibly a priest, wearing a garment with a distinctive trefoil design (fig. 4). Whether the relief carving of the garment was intended to depict woven, printed or embroidered fabric, this sculpture confirms that patterned cloth was in use in the Indus Valley at this early date.

The cotton found at Mehrgarh and Mohenjodaro is of an indigenous type (*Gossypium arboreum*) that required a long period of cultivation. It was only with the appearance of a more easily grown annual form (*Gossypium herbaceum*) in about the sixth or seventh century AD that cotton cultivation began to spread

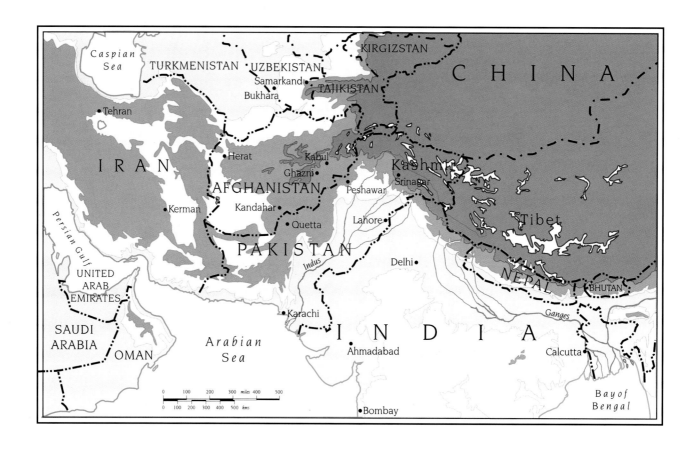

beyond its immediate area of origin and to become a major textile material outside the Indian subcontinent.[5] Even when the cultivation of the cotton plant became widespread, the secrets of dyeing the yarn with fast colours remained with the Indian dyers, who, at least as early as the Indus Valley period, had mastered the technique of using metallic salts as mordants to fix the dyes. They retained this supremacy until the introduction of artificial dyes in the late nineteenth century.

In addition to the extraordinary antiquity of the indigenous textile traditions of Pakistan, the designs, materials and techniques of the textiles made in the various regions have been very strongly influenced by the cultural changes brought about by successive influxes of outsiders. The whole of Pakistan has been subject to movement of people from the west (Iran, Afghanistan and Central Asia) towards India, and has also experienced continuous movement of population within its own boundaries, as a result of both seasonal nomadism and more permanent migrations (for example the annual movement of the Baluchis

TOP 1 The Indus in Skardu valley, Northern Areas, North-West Frontier Province, 1994 (Team Indus Expedition)

BELOW 2 Children playing by the banks of the parched Indus, where sheep provide sustenance and wool, near Sehwan, Kohistan, Sindh, 1995

3 Allan Faqir, a popular Sindhi folk singer, wearing an *ajrak* turban (*patko*), an *ajrak* wrap and a woollen shawl (*khatho*), Lok Virsa Festival, Islamabad, 1996

and the settlement of many Baluch groups in Sindh) and more recently, after Partition in 1947, the influx of large numbers of Muslims from India. As with any boundaries created primarily on an administrative rather than a physical basis, there are many cases where cultural characteristics (including textile types) are not contained within one defined area: for example, the *phulkari* stitch is to be found in various forms throughout Punjab and North-West Frontier Province (NWFP), several embroidery stitches and designs are common to both Sindh and Baluchistan, and the weaving of *khes* fabric has been carried out in Sindh, Punjab and Baluchistan. Furthermore the borders defining the areas of Pakistan are of very recent origin: the Durand Line separating Pakistan from Afghanistan was drawn up only at the end of the nineteenth century, while the eastern border with India was created in 1947 and in some areas is still under dispute. Until very recently, Powindahs (nomads) from Afghanistan and Iran travelled every year across the border into NWFP, parts of Punjab and Baluchistan. Many tribal groups on the Pakistan side have branches in Afghanistan, Iran and India, and it is frequently difficult – and sometimes impossible – to determine whether an object comes from one side of the border or the other.

As well as the continuous movement of peoples which dispersed indigenous textile techniques and patterns, more far-reaching influences have been exerted on the culture as a whole throughout Pakistan's history. Waves of Aryan peoples from Central Asia were entering Pakistan by around 1500 BC. The *Vedas*, texts compiled around 1500–1200 BC, refer to the use of many types of textile in cotton, silk

and wool, both woven and embroidered. From about 500 BC to AD 500, further incursions of northerners like the Scythians, Kushans and Huns may have brought the concept of stitched clothing to the area, perhaps as a consequence of their horse-riding culture which necessitated the use of trousers and jackets rather than draped garments. Written sources testify to a wide range of textiles in production by the last centuries BC,[6] and by the early centuries AD India as a whole was the hub of a vast textile trade which extended to the Mediterranean and China.

The coming of Islam to the region contributed immeasurably to its cultural development. The first Muslims to reach Pakistan were Arab traders, rapidly followed by invasion forces, who reached Sindh in AD 712, but the Islamic influence at this early period seems to have been confined to the southern area. (The fact that *ajrak*, the name of the resist-dyed cotton cloths of Sindh, may be derived from *azrak*, the Arabic word for blue, suggests that they could be a legacy of their presence there.)

Over the next four centuries, the area making up Pakistan, and Sindh in particular, became home to large numbers of migrants from the north-west and gradually developed into an important area of trade and production. Towns such as Thatta, Hyderabad (Nehrankot), Nasarpur, Sehwan, Rohri and Shikarpur developed as centres of craftsmanship as artisans from Iran, the Levant and Central Asia began to develop repertoires of *kasabnamahs* – collections of

4 Steatite figure of a man, possibly a priest, from Mohenjodaro, *ca.* 2000 BC (National Museum of Pakistan, Karachi 50.852.DK 1909). The trefoil pattern on the man's garment may have been intended to represent embroidery.

rhymes and songs relating to the origins of their crafts, the tools of their trades, patron saints, and other pieces of practical knowledge for daily practice.[7]

The most significant of the early incursions by Central Asian Turks was that of Mahmud of Ghazni (*died* AD 1030), whose empire extended as far east as Peshawar and Punjab. The Arghuns (AD 1521–54) and the Tarkhans (AD 1554–91), also of Central Asian origin, were patrons of the arts and ruled over the Lower Indus Valley until the Mughal emperor Akbar added it to his empire in 1592. The Mughals were the most enduring of the invaders of the subcontinent; their empire lasted from 1526 until 1858. Their legacy in Pakistan can be seen today most visibly in the great buildings of Lahore, which was the Mughal capital under the emperor Akbar from 1584 to 1598 and continued as one of the major centres of Mughal culture under his descendants Jahangir and Shah Jahan. The Mughal aesthetic, with its elegant floral and geometric decoration, is still evident in all media in Pakistan from architecture to textiles, and has provided the predominant design repertoire for all types of handicraft in urban Pakistan since the sixteenth century (see fig. 8). During the Mughal period, Lahore was a major centre for the production of textiles of many types and also of magnificent carpets which were made for the Mughal emperors from Akbar onwards. The *A'in-i Akbari*, the chronicle of Akbar's reign, recounts how the emperor set up carpet workshops to rival those of Iran and Turkestan in several centres, particularly Agra, Fatehpur and Lahore.[8] The carpets made there would almost certainly have been based on Persian prototypes to begin with, but a typical Mughal style of carpet evolved which has been linked specifically to Lahore, partly by virtue of labels bearing the attribution *Lahori* attached to several floral-patterned rugs now in Jaipur palace.[9] The rugs attributed to Lahore typically have a red ground patterned with rows of single flowering plants; other extraordinarily fine Mughal carpets made during the seventeenth century may also have been made there,[10] but no documentary evidence for this has yet come to light (see fig. 9). These fine carpets use *pashmina* – Kashmir goat's hair – for their pile rather than the coarser sheep's wool, and the availability in Lahore of weavers of *pashmina* for shawls may have

5 Mahar girls weaving a woollen floor rug (*farasi*), Khorwah, Badin, 1996

6 A traditional *khes* weaver, Nasarpur, Sindh, 1995

7 A carved stone column from Issa Khan Tarkhan's tomb, Thatta, Sindh, *ca.* 1574. The Tarkhans were Central Asian Turks who ruled over Sindh from 1554 to 1591 AD. Patterns similar to those on this column are found on printed, quilted and embroidered textiles throughout Sindh.

been a reason to weave the carpets there.

As well as carpets, Akbar had a considerable personal interest in clothing and textiles, and the *A'in-i Akbari* goes into some detail about the fabrics and costumes he kept in his store-rooms. Several types of textile from Lahore are specifically listed in the chronicle – brocaded velvet (under "gold stuffs"); velvet (plain); and scarlet broadcloth[11] – but it is probable that many more types of cloth, including silk brocades, would have been woven in the city.

The carpets made in Lahore appealed to the representatives of the British East India Company as well as the Mughal nobility, both as items of trade and for personal commissions. William Fremlin, a high-ranking representative of the Company based in Surat, had a carpet woven in Lahore in about 1640 with his family crest incorporated into the design (see fig. 10), and Robert Bell, a Director of the East India Company, had one woven with the arms of the Girdlers' Company alongside his own.[12] Lahore carpets, as well as those from Agra, were being exported to Britain from Surat as early as 1615,[13] and thirty Lahore carpets appear in the East India Company records in 1625 as exports to London.[14]

The East India Company had been established in 1600 and was quick to build up a presence in what is now Pakistan. Having opened an office in Surat in Gujarat in 1608, the Company opened a Sindh factory (trading centre) at Thatta on the Indus in 1635, following the destructive famine that befell Gujarat in 1630.[15] In spite of the famine, however, Surat rather than Thatta was to remain the major trading centre

for the Company in western India. Company records from the seventeenth century onwards, while mostly focussing on Surat and Cambay for the area, frequently refer to Sindh (and, to a lesser extent, Lahore) as centres of textile production, and list textiles that can be identified with fabrics still woven today in many parts of Pakistan, for example, *soosi*, *khes* and *ajrak*. Blue-and-white "keeses" (presumably the woven *khes* of Sindh and Punjab) were being exported from Surat by 1625, before the establishment of the Thatta factory.[16] Other types of cloth recorded as being manufactured in Sindh are less easy to identify, as they are rarely given any description in the records. One class of fabric mentioned frequently from 1609 to 1707 is termed *bafta*, which simply means 'woven' in Persian, and seems to have encompassed a wide range of quality and appearance of cloth. The earliest mentioned *baftas* are from Gujarat, but they also became a staple of the Sindh trade, and those from Nasarpur and Darbelo became known by their local names, *joories* and *dorbellas*.

Also mentioned in the report from Sindh in 1635 are "cambooles", which may perhaps be identified with the woollen blankets called *kambal* or *kambli* still made today. Another fabric described at that time is "a coarse sort of ginghams, which they call seriaes [also found elsewhere as 'seryas'], made of purpose for sails, of double thread".[17] A type of silk cloth woven in Sindh called "sabone" or "saboonees" is listed in 1645 and 1647, and in both cases its extreme popularity in Persia is commented on.[18]

8 Mughal tilework in Wazir Khan's mosque of 1634 in Lahore. Motifs such as the arabesque and the flowering tree have been components of the visual arts in Pakistan from the Mughal period to the present day.

9 Mughal carpet, probably made in Lahore, mid 17th century (Metropolitan Museum of Art, New York 1970.321). Clumps of flowers set against a plain background were the most popular design motif of Shah Jahan's reign (1628–58) and are seen in carpets and textiles as well as metalwork and on the borders of album pages. This carpet was formerly in the collection of the Maharajas of Jaipur and it bore a label stating that it was purchased from Lahore in 1066 AH (AD 1656).

Embroideries from Sindh had been known and admired by visitors since Marco Polo's day. The embroidered leather mats (*nat*) that are still used in Sindh today (see fig. 11) seem to have made a particular impression on European travellers and traders. In about 1585, the Dutch traveller Linschoten wrote that Sindh "hath most excellent and fair leather, which are most workmanlike and cunningly wrought with silk of all colours, both flowers and personages, this leather is in India much esteemed, to lay upon the beds and tables instead of carpets".[19] In 1641, the Augustine friar Sebastien Manrique remarked on these silk-embroidered leather mats, and noted that they were also made into elaborate horse-trappings.[20]

The British East India Company began to export embroideries from this region, on cloth rather than leather, in the 1690s. In 1695, we find from Sindh and Multan "quilting stitched very fine upon fine white cloth, both white and upon all other colours. Calico or silk finely embroidered according to the Country [that is, local] fashion."[21]

Sindh and the Punjab continued to be major textile producers throughout the eighteenth and nineteenth centuries, but with the introduction of new technology in the British textile industry in the nineteenth century exports from India fell off dramatically.

Nineteenth- and early twentieth-century observers of textile production in India now started to take note of different types of material. In 1856 John Forbes Watson, in his massive compilation of samples which he intended as a comprehensive "museum of manufacture", represented Lahore shawls, *khes*, splendid silk *lungis* and block-printed cottons as representative products of Sindh and Punjab (see fig. 12). International exhibitions which included Indian textiles brought to the attention of British commentators and the British public many types of textile normally seen only within a domestic context. These included embroideries from Punjab, the Frontier areas and Baluchistan, all of which gained recognition for the fineness of their stitches and their use of colour. George Watt, in his catalogue to the exhibition of Indian Art held in Delhi in 1903, mentions Hazara *phulkaris* as "specially worthy of study" and also praises Baluch embroidery.[22] Watt follows earlier commentators in his admiration for embroidery on

10 Detail of the Fremlin Carpet, Lahore, *ca.* 1640 (Victoria and Albert Museum IM1-1936). It was made for the East India Company official William Fremlin, whose family coats-of-arms are woven into the design.

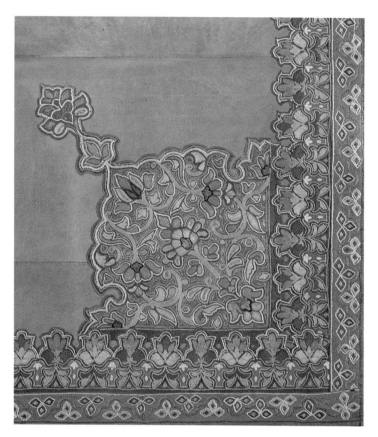

11 Detail of embroidered leather mat (*nat*) from Sindh, *ca*. 1855 (Victoria and Albert Museum IS 4730). Embroidery on leather had been admired by European visitors to Sindh as early as the sixteenth century.

leather, singling out a sword belt from the Dera Ghazi Khan area as "perhaps the most wonderful and elaborate needlework met with anywhere in India" (see fig. 120).[23]

The textiles so admired by Watt in 1903 were part of the last phase of hand-weaving, embroidery and printing in the subcontinent. The developments in technology and trade that were to take place during the twentieth century meant that there was no longer a place for the huge scale of manufacture by hand that had been the mainstay of the Indian textile industry. Socio-political change, leading up to the massive upheavals of Partition in 1947, saw the effective end of much of the embroidery that had once played such an important part in the domestic life of the subcontinent. The mass movements of people in 1947 had a significant impact on the textile traditions of both India and Pakistan. The major urban centres of Pakistan received an unprecedented influx of Muslim craftsmen from north India and the traditions of Mughal embroidery that had been their preserve survive today in the workshops of Karachi and Lahore. In addition to this cross-fertilization, independence brought with it urban growth and industrialization, together with the gradual erosion of the proprietory pride that had kept individual craftsmanship alive through the generations. Inevitably, this meant that the traditional commitment to workmanship diminished. Today, hand-made textiles are mostly restricted to the élite in Pakistan, although traditional weaving, printing and folk embroidery is still done in diminishing pockets in rural areas.

12 A page from J. Forbes Watson's eighteen-volume *Textile Manufactures of India*, London 1867 (III, no. 116), showing a sample of *khes* from Nurrapore (Nasarpur), Sindh. Forbes Watson's work was the first systematic attempt to document the range of textiles produced in the subcontinent.

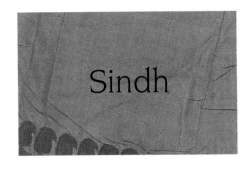

Sindh

Sindh, the southernmost province of Pakistan (population 35 million), comprises the Lower Indus Valley and the delta of the Indus at the Arabian Sea (see map overleaf). Its varied topography has led to the development of a number of costume traditions and extraordinary styles of decorating cloth. The central irrigated plains, Vicholo, are populated by a mixture of farming and fishing groups who excel at dyeing, printing and weaving. The Katcho plain (between the west bank of the Indus and the Kirthar and Lakhi ranges of Baluchistan) and Kohistan (literally 'hilly country', comprising the Kirthar Mountains on Sindh's western border) are home to a number of Baluchi mountain dwellers who have brought with them traditions of finely embroidered geometric patterns using mirrors (shisho). The northern plains, Siro, abutting on the Punjab, are known for their gold thread embroideries, dhagay jo bhart. The pakkoh and kacho, or soof, embroideries from Tharparkar, in Sindh's eastern corner, are among the most compelling in Pakistan, with bold, stylized motifs of dunes, flowers and peacocks drawn from nature. The deltaic lowlands, Larh, with their medieval capital at Thatta, cover the entire gamut of textile traditions — woven, printed, embroidered and quilted — for which Sindh was once renowned.

In addition to folk textiles such as these, Sindh's cities have developed dress traditions reflecting centuries of migration, trade and varied political influence. These range from elaborately worked and printed costumes that are a direct legacy of Mughal court designs, produced by professional artisans who migrated from India in 1947, to plain hand-loom and commercially manufactured cloth for tunics and trousers (shalwar kameez), worn throughout the country.

Folk Embroidery The folk embroideries of Sindh are among the richest in South Asia. Traditional costumes, accessories and animal adornments embroidered by women for their families are still in use among a number of groups scattered throughout the province. Although these textiles may have techniques, design elements and uses in common, many are peculiar to individual communities and distinguishable by their style, motifs and colour.

Tharparkar (see fig. 21) is part of a rambling desert that stretches over southern Punjab, north-west Rajasthan and Kutch.[1] It is one of the most inhospitable and least developed areas of Pakistan but continues to produce some of its most spectacular folk embroideries. The majority of its inhabitants are tightly knit groups of nomadic pastoralists, artisans and farmers, predominantly Muslim and Hindu. Muslim groups include the Soomrahs, Sammats,

13 Camel market (*maalpirhi*) outside Hala, Hyderabad, 1995

14 Kohli woman working in a field of sugar cane, Jati, Badin, 1995

15 Detail of tie-dyed embroidered skirt (*parha*), Lohana group, probably from Diplo, Tharparkar, early 20th century (Victoria and Albert Museum IS 6-1981; gift of Mrs Shireen Feroze Nana, Karachi). Tie-dyed, handspun cotton, silk embroidery and mirrors. W. 260 cm, H. 73 cm.

Sammahs, Jats, Langhas, Odhejas, Halepotas, Noorhias, Khojas, Khaskelis, Junejos, Memons and the Baloch (made up of a number of subgroups). The Hindu castes are primarily divided into the Brahmans, Lohanas, Maheshwaris, Rajputs, Ahirs, Thakurs, Jats, Odhs, Bajeers, Suthars, Meghwars, Saamis, Rabaris, Bhardwahs, Dheds, Bhils and Kohlis, each with their own traditions of cloth adornment. Textiles function as a non-verbal form of communication and, when decorated, as protective talismans. Motif, colour and composition signify an individual's group identity and occupation and, very often, social status. This is particularly the case for women, as in many parts of Tharparkar a woman who is unmarried, has children or who is widowed is immediately distinguishable by the ornaments she wears and by the shawl covering her head and shoulders.

Against the landscape of barren dun-coloured sand the Tharri woman presents an anthology of vibrant colour: a magnificent cotton blouse with an embroidered front (*gaj*), usually worn with a long voluminous skirt of gathered cotton, a *parha* or *gaghra* (see fig. 15), often dyed a deep red or black and anchored at the waist by a drawstring. The skirt may be embellished with a block-print, tie-dye or embroidery, while in some groups gathered trousers (*shalwar*) may be worn in its place. Over her head and back she wears an *odhani*, a large tie-dyed, block-printed or embroidered shawl often made of a lightweight cotton.[2] These three main articles of clothing are essential daily wear, but variations on this uniform theme are countless, according to the decorative styles of each group and individual creativity.

The *bhart* or embroideries of Tharparkar are found in two basic styles, the *pakkoh* and the *kacho* or *soof*. *Pakkoh* is a style of dense, heavily worked embroidery that has historically been linked to the areas surrounding Diplo and Mithi in central Tharparkar. The patterns are usually stamped on to cloth using carved wooden blocks (*por*) dipped in a paste made from soot, mud or powdered resin dissolved in water. *Pakkoh* embroidery consists of combinations of closely packed double-buttonhole, square-chain, interlaced square-chain, couched, satin and stem stitches, with accents in interlacing and cretan stitches. Small mirrors are usually attached in a tight double-buttonhole stitch and provide focal points in the overall pattern. Originally, pieces of naturally occurring mica were used but now mirrored glass is specially manufactured. The ground cotton or silk is usually lined and almost entirely covered with embroidery. Very often, when the silk has worn away the stitches remain intact, hence the name *pakkoh*, literally 'solid' or 'permanent'.

The *kacho* or *soof* style, which originated with the Sodha Rajputs in the thirteenth century,[3] relies on the counting of threads in the ground fabric. Satin stitches, usually put in from the reverse side, lie flat on the surface, and the forms produced bear a spatial relationship to one another. The motifs are not generally marked out on the fabric, although threads are occasionally drawn out to delineate areas to be filled in. Patterns worked in the *soof* style usually have the ground fabric visible between motifs that are immaculately constructed from fine geometric shapes (see fig. 19). *Soof* embroidery is also seen in conjunction with a stem or honeycomb

16 Baby's cap (*topi*), Memon group, Diplo, Tharparkar, mid 20th century (collection N. Askari). Cotton embroidered with silk and cotton, beads, tassels and a central silk tuft. H. 7 cm, diam. 11.5 cm.

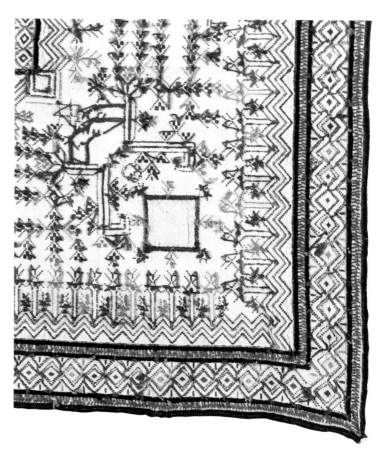

Detail of the reverse of fig. 19

17 Horse's head-cover (*aandheri*), Palli or Bhanbra group, Kadhan, Badin, mid 20th century (collection N. Askari). Cotton embroidered with silk and cotton, beads, tufts and tassels. L. 39 cm, W. 39 cm.

18 Coin purse (*kothri*), Meghwar or Noorhi group, Mithi, Tharparkar, early 20th century (collection N. Askari). Cotton with silk embroidery, mirrors, tassels and string. L. 56.5 cm, W. 9.2 cm.

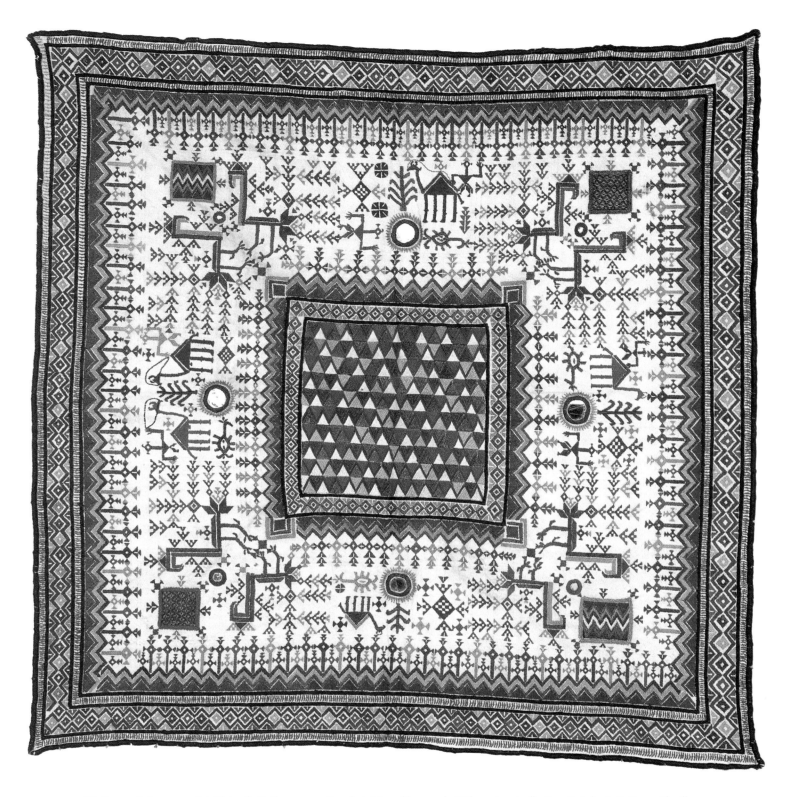

19 Dowry cloth or coverlet (*thalposh*), Suthar group, Umarkot, Mirpurkhas, early 20th century (collection N. Askari). Cotton with silk embroidery and mirrors. L. 40 cm, W. 42 cm. The intricate patterning on this coverlet from a group of traditional wood craftsmen is executed in the *kacho* or *soof* style of embroidery. The skilful use of surface darning stitches using a thread-counting technique has created a number of fine geometric shapes and motifs of flowers, human figures, camels, peacocks and scorpions.

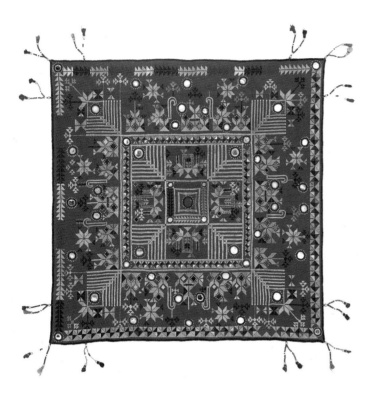

20 Dowry cloth or coverlet (*thalposh*), Suthar or Thakur group, Samaro, Mirpurkhas, early 20th century (collection N. Askari). H. 45 cm, W. 45 cm. The iconography of Tharparkar is immediately apparent in the composition of the embroidery. Four pairs of peacocks placed symmetrically in the central and outer fields with their plumage unfurled symbolize the newlyweds for whom this coverlet would have been made.

FACING PAGE 22 Details of men's wedding scarves or sashes (*bokano*). Left: Tando Bago, Badin, Larh, early 20th century (collection N. Askari). Cotton with silk embroidery. L. 131 cm, W 12.5 cm. Middle: Suthar group, Mirpurkhas or Tharparkar, mid 20th century (Victoria and Albert Museum, IS 16.1981; gift of Mrs Shireen Feroze Nana, Karachi). Cotton with silk embroidery, metal spangles, tassels and drawn thread work. L. 166 cm, W. 18 cm. Right: Meghwar group, Mithi, Tharparkar, early 20th century (collection Mr and Mrs F.S. Aijazuddin). Cotton with silk embroidery and mirrors. L. 164 cm, W. 17.5 cm. This superbly embroidered scarf combines the entire range of stitches used in traditional *pakkoh* embroidery.

filling, interlacing and buttonhole stitches and mirrors. The Suthars, a group of artisans traditionally associated with wood crafts in Tharparkar, are especially renowned for the whimsical *soof* patterns which they carry over on to carved utilitarian wooden objects such as saddles, tools, farming implements, mortars and bowls. The Suthar women's ingenuity in embroidering and combining simple shapes to depict natural forms finds ultimate expression in the garments they prepare as dowry gifts for their daughters and sons-in-law. Mirrors, cotton thread and floss silk are commonly used; where satin stitches are laid out on the surface of the cloth and

not visible on the reverse (as in a false-satin or surface darning stitch), the embroidery is referred to as *kachi tand soof* (one-sided) whereas stitches visible on both sides are referred to as *hakim* or *paki tand soof* (two-sided).

The peacock found all over Tharparkar is the leitmotif of its embroidered textiles. Among the Hindu Meghwar groups, who are professional embroiderers, leather workers, tanners, builders and farmers, the peacock is a metaphor for a bridegroom who comes to claim his bride from her parents. The long narrow scarf, *bokano*, that he is given by his future mother-in-law for his wedding day has a fanciful design of peacocks among flowers and on top of hills or dunes (see fig. 22). The peacock is revered as a noble bird, it is the embodiment of good and is often represented as a vehicle for Saraswati, goddess of wisdom, poetry and the arts. Peacocks, as Tharri folk legends relate, are thought not to mate physically but through the medium of dance. The highly stylized pairs of birds depicted along the length of the groom's *bokano* symbolize the coming together of the newlyweds and the sanctity of their union. They are embroidered in a row of symmetrical rectangles alternating with columns of flowers and mirrors that run along the entire length of the scarf. A longer and broader version of the *bokano*, the *karhbandhro*, is used by Rajput, Thakur and Meghwar bridegrooms as a cummerbund for their loincloths (*threto*). It may be wound tightly around the waist several times, and knotted with the embroidered ends left hanging down (see fig. 25).

Flowers symbolizing fertility and prosperity for the bridal couple are found in practically all Tharparkar

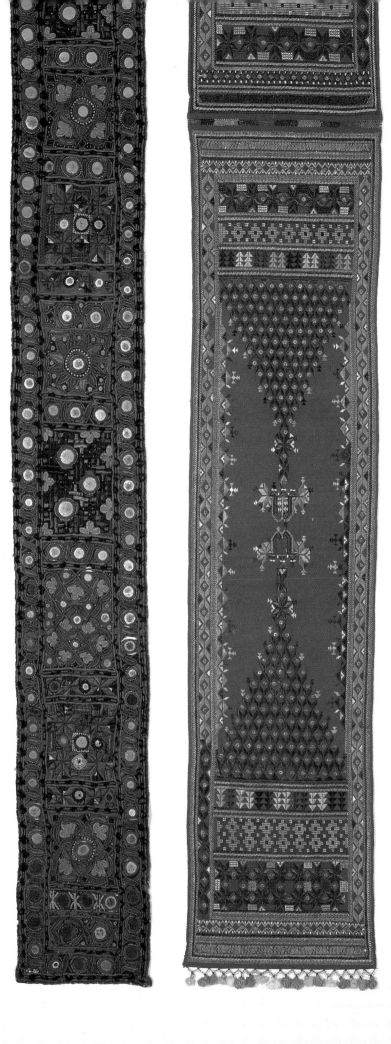

23 A *rohirho* tree (*Techoma undulaca*) in full bloom following the annual monsoon. Kasbo village, Nagarparkar, Tharparkar, 1993

FACING PAGE 24 Woman's tunic (*cholo*), Meghwar group, Jehpoyo, Tharparkar, early 20th century (collection N. Askari). Silk lined with cotton, silk-thread embroidery, mirrors, silk tufts, coloured silk tassels and ties. L. 87 cm, W. 44 cm. The unusual construction of this garment suggests that it may have been specially commissioned from Meghwar embroiderers; the blouse front (*gaj*) has a large apron (*peyti*) added to it at the front with pieced back panels .

wedding garments. The largest and most outstanding of these is the Meghwar man's wedding shawl or *doshalo*, a large mordant-dyed and resist-printed cotton shawl or *maleer* embroidered in the *pakkoh* style by the bride and her family for her wedding day (see fig. 26). The *doshalo* and *bokano* often share a decorative theme of peacocks, and are made up of two symmetrical halves of cloth joined by a web of fine interlacing stitches called a *kheelo*. The *doshalo* is usually elaborately embroidered at its ends and has densely embroidered squares resembling flower beds at the four corners. It is thrown around a bridegroom's shoulders by his female relatives as he leaves to collect his bride on their wedding day, and he continues to wear it with the ends thrown forward over his shoulders for the journey and rituals that will follow at the bride's house. Occasionally it may be wound flamboyantly around his head in the form of a turban with the ends hanging down over his shoulders. When he is finally allowed to leave with his bride, the *doshalo* is symbolically draped around them both, each holding one end. Among some Meghwar families the *doshalo* is hoisted like a canopy over the newlyweds, its corners usually held by close male relatives of the bride as she takes leave of her parents. It is a treasured dowry gift and continues to be used as a shawl or spread on auspicious occasions throughout the couple's life.

The flowers represented on the Meghwar *doshalo* and *bokano* are usually renditions of desert flowers, most commonly the *golharho* (*Coccinia cordifolia*) and *rohirho* (*Techoma undulaca*; fig. 23), embroidered in the *pakkoh* style using combinations of elongated square-chain, interlaced square-chain, double-buttonhole and satin stitches (see fig. 24). Accents may be added in satin, pattern-running or fly stitches (*chanwar kani*). The flowers are predominantly red, orange and white floss (untwisted) silk or cotton thread with centrally placed mirrors. Accompanying green, purple and yellow leaves are very often outlined in black stem and white back or couched stitches. As a particular printed and embroidered textile is part of the groom's wedding accessories, the bride's *abochhini* or shawl (see figs. 27, 28, 29) is also embroidered in a characteristic style and distribution of motifs (*buti*). Among the farming and semi-nomadic groups in

Tharparkar and the adjoining areas of the Indus delta, the Sammat, Memon, Lohana, Khaskeli, Baloch and Soomrah, bridal shawls usually have scattered buds or blossoms of the *akk* plant (*Calotropia procera*) embroidered in pink or red floss silk in a typical *phulhri* or herringbone stitch for the petals and a green floss silk in chain or square-chain stitches for the leaves.[4] Other stylized flowering plants such as the *beyri* (*Zizyphus jujuba*), the *kanwal* or lotus (*Sindica nymphia*) and the *pat kanwar* (*Malva parviflora*) are depicted in a unique scatter pattern either as single flowers or as clusters placed in rows around an elaborate central medallion (see fig. 30). Half medallions along the upper and lower edges with quarter medallions at the corners and end borders enclosing clumps of flowers are also particular features.

The costumes and textiles of the frontier herding groups in Tharparkar are among the most powerful because of the symbiosis over many centuries of Muslim and Hindu social and religious traditions. Amongst these, the Muslims attach a great deal of importance in girls to appliqué, quilting and embroidery skills, which are in direct proportion to their desirability as wives and mothers. Conventional wisdom dictates that girls begin to accumulate and work on their dowries when very young as they should include a variety of clothing: several blouse-fronts, a skirt, storage bags, purses, dowry wraps, a quilt and as much jewellery as their fathers can afford.[5]

Among the herdsmen who live close to the border with India and who earn their keep by selling supplies

25 Man's ceremonial cummerbund (*karhbandhro*), Rajput, Thakur or Meghwar group, probably Chachro, Tharparkar, early 20th century (collection Mr and Mrs F.S. Aijazuddin). Cotton with silk embroidery and mirrors, beads and tassels. L. 384 cm, W. 56 cm.

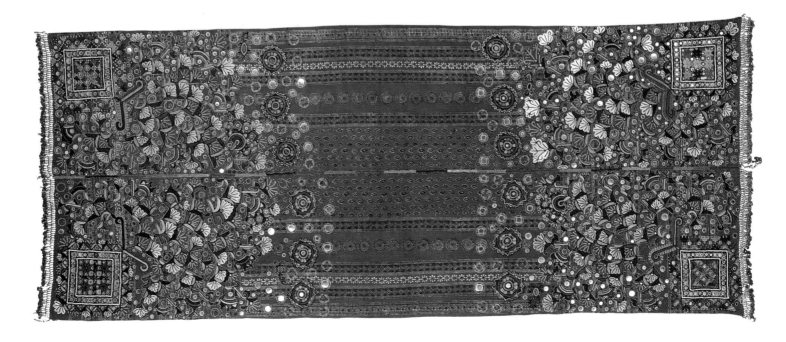

27 Woman's shawl (*abochhini*), probably Memon group, Badin, Larh, late 19th to early 20th century (Victoria and Albert Museum IS 19-1957). Silk, with silk embroidery. L. 193 cm, W.135 cm. See also detail overleaf.

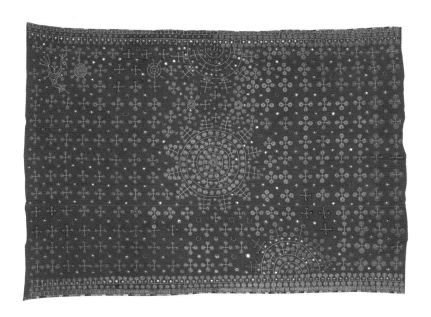

28 Woman's shawl (*abochhini*), probably Khaskheli group, Sanghar, Vicholo, early 20th century (collection Mr and Mrs F.S. Aijazuddin). Cotton with silk embroidery and mirrors. L. 206 cm, W. 147.5 cm. The flowering motifs may represent peacock feathers and the top left-hand corner shows an encounter between a peacock and a scorpion. See also detail overleaf.

RIGHT 29 Woman's shawl (*abochhini*), Sammat group, Jhudo or Mohrano, border of Badin and Tharparkar, *ca*. mid 20th century (Victoria and Albert Museum IS 9-1981; gift of Mrs Shireen Feroze Nana, Karachi). Cotton with silk embroidery and mirrors. L. 210 cm, W. 166.5 cm. This shawl from a Muslim farming group illustrates the style and distribution of embroidered floral motifs seen on wedding shawls throughout the delta and desert areas. See also detail overleaf.

LEFT 26 Man's wedding shawl (*doshalo*), Meghwar group, probably Diplo, Tharparkar, early 20th century (Victoria and Albert Museum IS 7-1981; gift of Mrs Shireen Feroze Nana, Karachi). Handspun and woven cotton, mordant-dyed and resist-printed *maleer* with silk embroidery, mirrors, beads and silk tassels. L. 276 cm, W. 106 cm. This splendid shawl would be a gift from a Meghwar bride and her family to the groom for his wedding-day attire. The design, symbolizing fertility and prosperity for the bridal couple, shows stylized peacocks among fields of desert flowers and flower beds at the four corners.

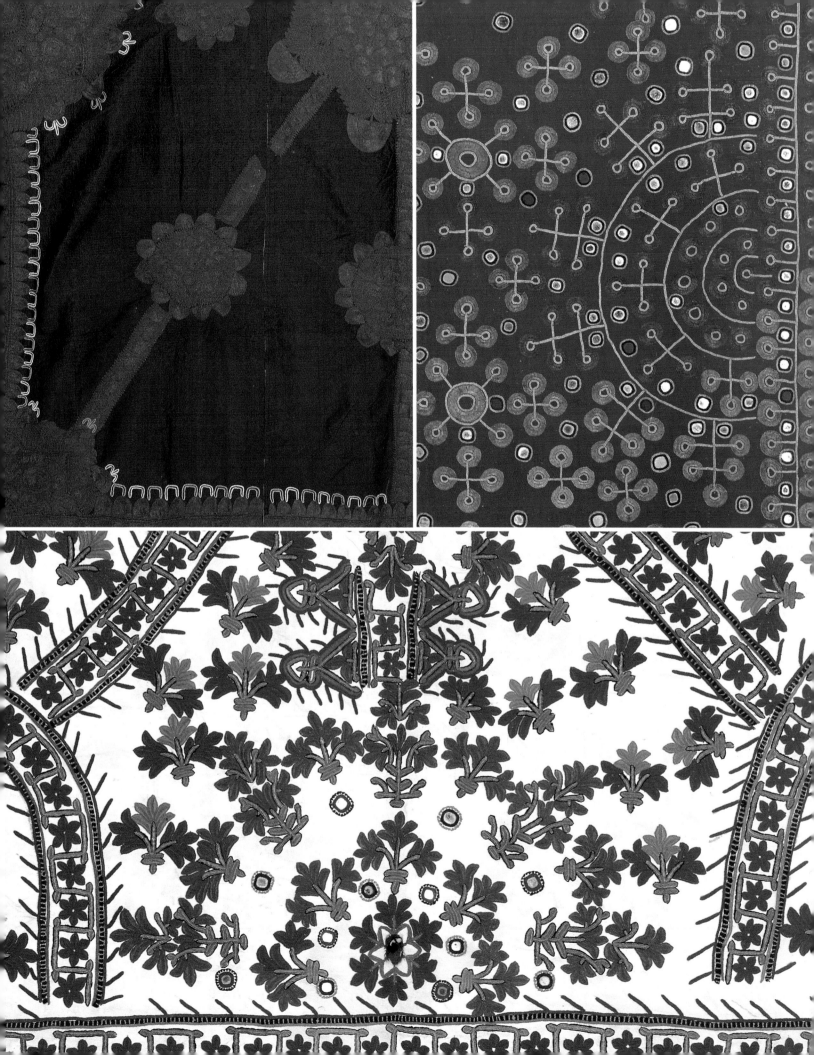

30 Woman's shawl (*abochhini*), probably Sammat group, Tharparkar, *ca*. mid 20th century (Victoria and Albert Museum IS 10-1981; gift of Mrs Shireen Feroze Nana, Karachi). Cotton with silk embroidery and mirrors. L. 184 cm, W. 145.5 cm.

FAR LEFT TOP Detail of fig. 27   LEFT TOP Detail of fig. 28   LEFT BELOW Detail of fig. 29

of milk and *ghee* (clarified butter used as a cooking medium) or as artisans and labourers in neighbouring towns and farms, the Rabaris are particularly well known for their spirited embroideries. The women's veils (*odhani*) and gathered skirts (*gaghra*) are black to symbolize a state of ritual mourning.[6] Wool is most commonly used and is of a coarse handspun variety (see fig. 31) as it is the most cost-effective and readily available raw material. The woollen cloth may have a simple woven black-and-white chequer-board pattern, or it may be left plain or tie-dyed before it is embroidered. A distinctive Kutchi Rabari textile is the dark woollen *ludi* or *odhani* that girls embroider for their weddings. It has a tie-dyed pattern of red, orange or yellow dots, and is elaborately embroidered at both ends and along a central seam with scattered medallions of one of the vividly coloured desert flowers of which the most popular is a bright-yellow mimosa (*Acacia arabica*). With all Rabari motifs there is very little distinction between representation and abstraction. The stylized flowers, symbols of fertility, often have raised centres using triangular-shaped mirrors and white buttons as accents. The ends, often with a supplementary weft pattern, have dramatic embroideries of flowers and peacocks in square-chain, interlacing, herringbone, buttonhole and

couched stitches (see fig. 33). At the same time the bridegroom carries a brightly embroidered *pothu* or purse edged with coloured felted-wool pompons (see fig. 32) as he travels with his family and friends to his bride's house, echoing the vibrant colours and embroidery in yellow, white, pink, orange, green and purple thread on her *ludi*.

Larh, the low-lying delta areas of the Indus, are home to groups of Jat nomads, regarded as camel breeders of Scythian extraction and amongst the oldest inhabitants of Sindh.[7] Today, Jat groups are found all over Sindh but large groups of Malkani, Nuhani, Jumani, Faqirani and Umrani Jats who continue to breed buffalos, camels and other livestock in Badin and along its western border with Tharparkar have also taken to farming. The women's costumes of the different groups share basic design elements or motifs that have identical names as they are commonly both drawn from nature and reflect the gradual transition from a nomadic to an agrarian way of life. Stylized forms of the sun, moon, stars, flowers, streams, rice grains, millet stalks and fields of crops are reduced and repeated to form ingenious minimalist patterns used in striking juxtapositions. Mirrors highlighting individual motifs can vary in size from tiny imperceptible dots to pear-shaped discs of up to

31 Rabari man spinning wool, Aadhigaon, Tharparkar. Rabari (literally 'outside the way' or 'without') are groups of Hindu pastoralists who live in hamlets in the south-eastern areas of Tharparkar around Nagarparkar and along the Kutch border. As a result of their relative isolation and a strict adherence to group identity, they have maintained most of their textile traditions.

32 Bridegroom's purse (*pothu*), Kutchi Rabari group, near Kasbo village, Nagarparkar, Tharparkar, mid 20th century (private collection). Cotton embroidered with silk and cotton, mirrors, buttons, beads and felt balls. L. 28 cm, W. at bottom 33 cm. A Rabari bridegroom often carries small sweetmeats or betel-nut shavings in this purse to distribute to those participating in his wedding rituals.

33 Woman's shawl (*ludi*), Kutchi Rabari group, near Kasbo village, Nagarparkar, Tharparkar, mid 20th century (collection N. Askari). Wool, supplementary weft ends, tie-dyed and embroidered with silk and cotton, appliqué, mirrors, buttons and felt balls. L. including tassels 251 cm, W. 94.5 cm.

15 mm in diameter. The Jats are an imposing people who live and travel in tightly knit, independent groups headed by their leader, *malik*. Their women wear a *chori*, a long, full-skirted dress with gathered trousers (*shalwar*) and a large shawl (*odhani*). The *chori* reaches to the ankles and is finely pleated beneath the armholes, and the bodice is usually adorned with a *gaj*, referred to as a *giichi*. The form and colour of the *chori* indicates the woman's status, while her regional identity may be conveyed through the distribution of its motifs. Generally, red *choris* are worn by young girls, brides and women with a more fashionable bent (see figs. 34, 35), while widows and older women wear black *gaghos*, *choris* with less elaborately embroidered and mirrorless *gaj*. The *giichi* is embroidered in a meticulous grid layout that covers the chest almost entirely. This linear arrangement is a distinctive feature of Jat embroidery. The sun is a predominant motif framed by rows of stylized flowers in narrow borders or columns containing mirrors. The embroidery is less dense than the *pakkoh* style of Tharparkar, with combinations of square-chain, buttonhole, interlacing, satin and couched stitches using maroon, black, white and occasionally yellow-ochre silk or cotton thread. Symmetrically placed roundels embroidered in laid and couched stitches have triangular rays emanating from the centre. The edges of the *gaj*, the sleeves, the hem and the neckline together with its central opening are often fortified by a striking black cretan stitch, the *gaano*. Umrani Jat women often attach columns of tear-drop-shaped mirrors in bold red, black and white buttonhole stitches on to their yoke, with a scatter of floral motifs on their sleeves that reduce sequentially in size as they approach the cuffs. The cuffs of the sleeves end in a fixed combination of embroidered borders, *kungri*, *tikko*, *dor*, *warho* and finally the *gaano*.

Women of other settled farming and fishing groups in Larh who do not share the same origins as the Jats wear loose knee-length tunics, *cholo* or *kurto*, with striped *shalwars* and *odhanis*. The *gaj* is laid out within a framework of four symmetrical squares on the bodice and shoulders and a central column running down to end just above the stomach (see figs. 37, 44). These are first marked out with black thread and then filled in with embroidery in no fixed

34 A Faqirani Jat woman returning from a pilgrimage at the shrine of Ibrahim Shah Varhi Varo, patron saint of Jat herdsmen, Shah Bandar, Thatta, 1996. She is wearing a full-skirted dress (*chori*) with a richly embroidered front (*giichi*).

35 A Faqirani Jat woman wearing a beautiful tie-dyed shawl (*bandhani*) and a traditional gold nose-ring (*nuth*), outside Thatta, 1996

36 Devotional offerings at the shrine of Ibrahim Shah Varhi Varo, Shah Bandar, Thatta, 1996. These consist of an array of meticulously embroidered small blouse-fronts (*gaj*), squares, amulets and hangings tied by devotees and pilgrims as tokens of thanksgiving or vows in times of need.

TOP LEFT 37 Woman of the Meerbahar fishing group on her way to buy provisions, outside Haji Ahmed Sumar Goth, Badin, Larh, 1996. She is wearing a contemporary rendition of the traditional tunic (*cholo*), gathered trousers (*shalwar*) and a floral machine-printed shawl (*odhani*). She had already walked five miles from her village.

LEFT 38 A Jat woman of the Barjhang group of nomadic pastoralists cutting and carrying grass for her herd near Allahrakhio Shah, Thatta, 1996. The Barjhang Jats migrate seasonally through the plains and delta areas in search of pasture.

ABOVE 39 Quilted dowry bag (*gothro*), Tando Mohammed Khan, Vicholo, early 20th century (collection N. Askari). Bands of tie-dyed silk, printed and plain cotton with silk embroidery, mirrors, glass, beads, cowrie shells and silk tassels. L. 76 cm, W. 46 cm.

arrangement of forms or motifs. The colours are used in a vibrant *satrangi* ('seven colours') combination: red, green, orange, deep blue, white, yellow and black or purple. Although these *gaj* share a number of stitches with the *pakkoh* style and are essentially floral in theme, their edges are much more fluid and rounded. In addition to square-chain, double-buttonhole, herringbone, cretan and chain stitches, Romanian couching and a characteristic *kharek* (literally 'fruit of the date palm') stitch are commonly used. The *kharek* stitch is made up of narrow bars of satin stitch laid closely together in the form of tri-angles, V-shapes or small squares. Mirrors may be used as central highlights and when outlined with a couched stitch the *kharek* works effectively as an out-lining or as a filling-in stitch (see fig. 45); used in this way the bars of satin stitch are also known as *nehran* ('river'). These groups borrow freely and adapt designs from one another, so that it is often difficult for an outsider to identify a woman's clan by her *gaj*. Distinctions are also becoming increasingly blurred as costumes are being adapted to use less labour-intensive and more modern materials. Synthetic fab-rics and printed cottons that simulate traditional designs and motifs are very popular. Traditional *odhanis*, except for important social occasions and festivals (weddings, *urs* and *melas*), have largely been replaced by factory-printed floral fabric (see fig. 37).

For Jat women, dowry ritual garments often provide a more reliable guide. For seven days prior to the wedding (*vanah*) the bride wears a wedding mask or *akkheun* (literally 'eyes'; see fig. 41), an embroidered square- or triangular-shaped cloth which covers the upper half of her face almost entirely but enables her to see through perforations. The *akkheun* is a pre-amble to the moment her husband will catch his first glimpse of her face in a mirror that is held between them. This ritual of *munh disan*, or glimpsing the face, marks the beginning of *lavan* – the informal rites of marriage. The bride's *gaj* is frequently adorned with mirrors and intricate metallic-thread embroidery called *muka*. In some groups wheat stalks are treated with a vermilion dye and stitched on to blouse-fronts to simulate gold (*zari*) work.

The embroidered *gaj* of farming groups in the Vicholo or central plains near Nawabshah, Hala and

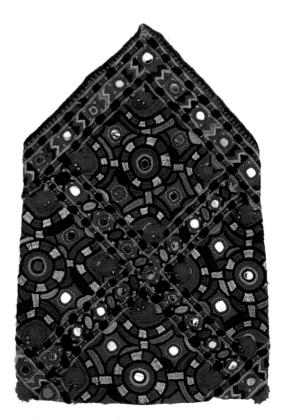

40 Dowry bag or purse (*bhujki*), Palli or Rajput group, Tando Allahyar Khan, Hyderabad, Vicholo, mid 20th century (private collection). Cotton with silk and cotton embroidery, mirrors and tassels. L. 38.5 cm, W. 26 cm.

41 Bridal face mask (*akkheun*), Jherruck, Thatta, mid 20th century (private collection). The design of this face mask is referred to as *chikri tik payo* ('stars and flowers'). L. 26 cm, W. 22 cm. It is worn by a bride for seven days preceding her wedding as she is prepared for the formal ceremonies. Its removal, when her groom first glimpses her face in a mirror on their wedding day, indicates the beginning of the informal rites of marriage.

42 Embroidered blouse-front (*gaj*), Kunbhar group, Badin or Tharparkar, mid 20th century (Sindh Provincial Museum, Hyderabad). Silk lined with cotton, silk embroidery with mirrors. L. 76 cm, W. 59 cm.

43 Embroidered blouse-front (*gaj*), Umrani Jat group, Jamali Shah village, Nawabshah, Vicholo, mid 20th century (collection N. Askari). Tie-dyed cotton, cotton lining, silk embroidery and mirrors. L. 70 cm, W. 76 cm.

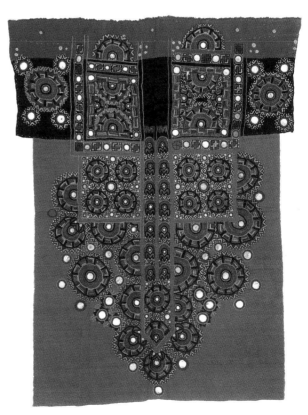

44 Embroidered blouse-front (*gaj*), Nindo Shehr, Badin, Larh, early 20th century (collection N. Askari). Green silk lined with cotton, silk embroidery with mirrors. L. 70 cm, W. 55 cm.

45 Embroidered blouse-front (*gaj*), Chetiari, Sanghar, Mohrano, mid 20th century (collection N. Askari). Tie-dyed cotton, cotton lining, cotton and silk embroidery and mirrors. L. 70 cm, W. 68 cm.

46 Child's embroidered silk dress (*angrakho*), Hyderabad, Vicholo, early 20th century (Victoria and Albert Museum IM 280-1920; Lady Ratan Tata Collection, Bombay). Silk lined with cotton, silk embroidery. L. 59 cm, W. across sleeves 86.5 cm.

47 Boy's embroidered tunic (*angrakho*), Rabari group, probably Matli, Badin Larh, early 20th century (Victoria and Albert Museum IS 18-1981; gift of Mrs Shireen Feroze Nana). Cotton embroidered with silk and applied mirrors. L. 66 cm, W. 87 cm.

48 Child's embroidered dress (*angrakho*), Hyderabad, Vicholo, early 20th century (Victoria and Albert Museum IS 139-1960). Silk with silk embroidery. L. 45 cm, W. across sleeves 54.5 cm.

49 Boy's ceremonial tunic (*kurta*), Shikarpur, Siro, early 20th century (Victoria and Albert Museum IS 58-1981). Embroidered silk. L. 82 cm, W. across sleeves 109 cm.

50 Girl's embroidered dress (*pairhan*), Soomro group, Jinaan Soomro village, near Sujawal, Badin, *ca.* 1954 (Sindh Provincial Museum, Hyderabad). Silk, lined with cotton, silk and gold-wrapped thread embroidery, metal spangles, silk and gold-thread braid and faceted glass beads. L. 83 cm, W. across sleeves 110 cm. Made to celebrate the betrothal and *aameen* ceremony of Ibrahim Munshi Soomro's daughter as she had finished reading the *Quran*. Gold-wrapped thread has been couched and finely worked in an auspicious necklace pattern (*haar*).

Hyderabad show a stunning range of both floral and geometric combinations (see figs. 46–50). The interlacing *hurmitch* stitch is often prominently used in combination with a double buttonhole for the mirrors, *hakim soof*, satin, couched, chain and stem stitches.[8] The embroideries of the north or Siro around Jacobabad, Shikarpur and Sukkur are more geometric, reflecting the diverse influences which these areas have enjoyed. Shikarpur has always acted as an entrepôt between the Upper and Lower Indus Valleys and along ancient trade routes between China, Central Asia, India and the Middle East.

Groups of Mahars, who like the Jats are pastoralists and cattle breeders, have taken to farming arable tracts around Shikarpur, Ghotki and along the Cholistan border. They combine exquisitely embroidered geometric and floral patterns with small mirrors (*shishobhart*). Mahar *thalposh* (ceremonial or dowry wraps), *chadars* (shawls) and *bhujkis* (purses) are immediately recognizable as the interlacing, double-buttonhole, square-chain, cross, couched and satin stitches are extraordinarily fine, and the curvilinear outlines seen in the *gaj* from further south are replaced by increasingly square and polygonal

51 Girl's embroidered dress (*pairhan*), Lohana, Pallari or Burfati group, Thano Bula Khan, Kohistan, early 20th century (collection N. Askari). Silk with silk and silver-thread embroidery, mirrors and metal spangles. L. 75 cm, W. across sleeves 72 cm.

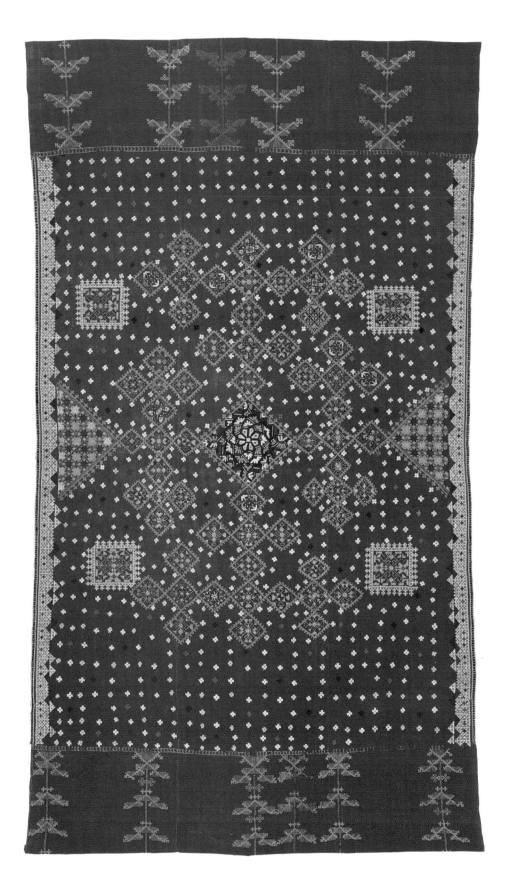

LEFT 52 Woman's shawl (*abochhini*), attributed to Mai Rani, Dooloh Faqir Mahar village, Ghotki, Sukkur, early 20th century (collection N. Askari). Handspun and hand-woven cotton with silk and cotton embroidery. L. 230 cm, W. 140 cm. Mahars in the north of Sindh embroider in a remarkable cross-over style combining decorative elements and stitches from Sindh with the fine geometric forms found in Baluchistan.

RIGHT ABOVE 53 Dowry bag (*bhujki*), Mahar group, Ghotki or Mirpur Mathelo, Sukkur, Siro, mid 20th century (collection S.J. Cohen). Cotton embroidered with silk and cotton, mirrors, cotton tassels and string. H. 27 cm, W. 19 cm.

RIGHT BELOW 54 Dowry cloth or coverlet (*thalposh*), Ali Buksh Mahar village, near Chanesar Goth, Daherki, Sukkur, mid 20th century (collection N. Askari). Cotton with silk and silver-thread embroidery, mirrors, glass beads and silk tassels. L. 84 cm, W. 88 cm.

FAR RIGHT ABOVE 55 Man's cap (*topi*), Dil Murad village, Jacobabad, 1995 (private collection). Cotton embroidered with silk and mirrors. H. 7 cm, diam. 16 cm.

FAR RIGHT BELOW 56 Boy wearing a Sindhi cap (*topi*), Kot Imamgarh, Khairpur, Siro, 1995

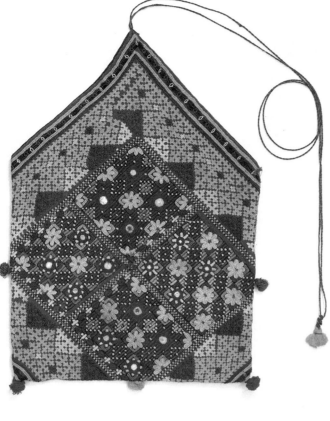

57 Khosa Baloch nomads on the move, Manjhand, Dadu, 1995. The men have gone on ahead to forage and have arranged to meet up with the women at a pre-appointed place.

compositions of embroidery (see figs. 52–54). The Sindhi cap (*topi*) from the Siro (see fig. 55) has the finest embroidery, using *pat* or silk thread with tiny mirrors. It has a flat crown and a soft, even rim with a dome-shaped cut-out over the forehead.

Areas of the Dadu district in the west of Sindh and the Katcho plain are inhabited by Sindhi Baloch groups – the Khosas, Palaris, Jokhias, Burfati and Karmatis, who live on both sides of the Kirthar and Lakhi ranges. Their *gaj* embroideries consist of intricate geometric patterns in the *soof* style. Mirrors are not generally used and individual motifs are framed in vertical columns. Of particular interest are the Lohana women of farming groups in Thano Bula Khan who embroider stunning silk *cholas*, straight knee-length tunics so thickly encrusted with panels of embroidery that the ground fabric is entirely stiff (see fig. 59). The *cholas* are wedding shirts, but similar densely structured embroidery using 'heaped' forms of double-buttonhole, square-chain and open-chain

58 Dowry bag or purse (*bhujki*), probably Jokhia Baloch group, Khairpur Nathan Shah, Dadu, mid 20th century (Victoria and Albert Museum IS 21-1981; gift of Mrs Shireen Feroze Nana, Karachi). Cotton with silk embroidery, mirrors, silk tassels, threads and beads. H. 35 cm, W. 19 cm.

61 Boy's cap (*topi*), Lohana, Pallari or Burfati group, Thano Bula Khan, Dadu, early 20th century (collection Zulfiqar Ali Shah Jamote). Silk embroidered with silk, sequins and mirrors.

59 Woman's tunic (*chola*), Lohana, Pallari or Burfati group, Thano Bula Khan, Dadu, mid 20th century (Victoria and Albert Museum IS 15-1974). Silk embroidered with silk, sequins, gold-wrapped thread and mirrors. L. 87 cm, W. 44 cm.

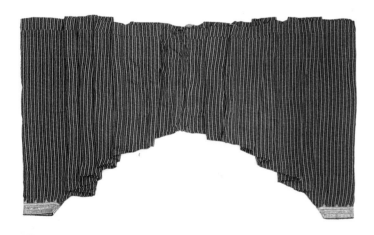

60 Striped cotton trousers (*suthan* or *shalwar*) with embroidered cuffs (*paincha*), Thano Bula Khan, Dadu, mid 20th century (collection H. Iwatate). L. 96 cm, W. 384 cm.

62 Camel saddle-cloth (*gaadi*), Lohana group, Thano Bula Khan, Dadu, early 20th century (Justice Feroze Nana Collection, Sindh Provincial Museum, Hyderabad). Silk lined with cotton, embroidered with silk and silver thread, mirrors, sequins and silk tassels. H. 78 cm, W. 76 cm.

63 Dowry cloth or coverlet (*thalposh*), probably Talhar, Badin, Larh, mid 20th century (collection N. Askari). Cotton with silk embroidery and mirrors. H. 60 cm, W. 60 cm.

65 Camel trapping (*jhul*), Rajput group, Golarchi, Badin, mid 20th century (collection N. Askari). Cotton and goat hair with woollen pompons and leather fastenings. L. 203 cm, W. of strap 12 cm.

64 Kohli women and children waiting for a bus outside Jamshoro, Hyderabad, 1994. Handspun and handwoven textiles have been superseded by factory-made fabric in and around many large towns.

66 Illustration to the romance of Dhola and Maru, Jodhpur, Rajasthan, mid 19th century (collection Sangram Singh), showing the lovers on a camel adorned with a *jhul* like that in fig. 65.

stitches are also used to embellish children's dresses (see fig. 51), caps (see fig. 61), coverlets and animal adornments (fig. 62).

Leather Embroidery Martin tells us that in 1903 Hyderabad was well known for its fine *mochi* (chain-stitch) leather embroidery on gaiters, camel saddle-covers, scabbards, sword belts, jesses and gauntlets for falconry, and that the import of cheap European leather was beginning to affect patronage and demand among the "Mirs, Pirs and Sayeds".[9]

Several Meghwar communities in Tharparkar today continue to make *nat* or camel-saddle cloths out of soft hog, deer or calf skin. These are embroidered with coloured silk as well as silver and gold thread. *Jootis*, or shoes, made of bullock or cow hide are in popular use. Except for those worn in Tharparkar and its extension (*aachro Thar*) into the Cholistan Desert of southern Punjab, Sindhi women's *jootis* are shaped like slippers with narrow tapering soles. *Jootis* from Kandhkot, Khairpur, Shikarpur and Jacobabad in the north are often made out of elaborately embroidered uppers of velvet lined with leather, using an awl or hooked needle. The best known are the tufted *jootis* (*tauranwari*) of central Sindh. Burton describes them as "a most inconvenient kind of shoe, consisting of a mere sole, scarcely covering the toes and presenting peculiar difficulties to the walker".[10] Depending on the pattern created in the tufted threads (see fig. 68) they are referred to as *kakkar* ('cloud'), *sath phul* ('seven flowers'), *tay phul* ('three flowers') or *khumchi* ('cluster').

Urban Embroidery Ornamental embroidery using coloured silks or silver- and gold-wrapped thread on fine muslin (*malmal*), cotton, silk, velvet and fine silk and gold weaves provides employment for large numbers of skilled craftsmen in workshops in Karachi, Hyderabad, Shikarpur, Khairpur and Jacobabad. In form, the embroidery combines styles and patterns ranging from the elaborate arabesques and flowering *butis* of the Mughal repertoire to adaptations of the robust colours and forms of folk embroidery. Mughal traditions of decorating textiles thrive in the larger urban centres of Karachi, Multan and Lahore because artisans take pride in the belief that they are heirs to

67 Camel saddle-cover (*nat*), Tando Jam, Hyderabad, Vicholo, mid 20th century (Sindh Provincial Museum, Hyderabad). L. 69 cm, W. 69 cm.

this genre of Muslim craftsmanship from north India.

Zardozi is a term used to describe the stitching or couching of silver and gold threads and wires of varying thickness and forms (*kalabatun*, *naqshi* and *dabka*) on to fabric stretched tightly over a wooden frame (*karchob*).[11] Silk thread, sequins (*sitara*), beads (*mothi*) and *gota* (ribbon-like strips woven from yellow silk and gold thread) are also used in conjunction with the wires to adorn ceremonial wear for men, women and children, velvet coverlets, hats (see fig. 74), purses and book covers (see fig. 73). Fine silver wire beaten into a flat ribbon (*badla* or *kamdaani*) is often used to decorate *saris*, *kurtas*, *shalwars* and *dupattas* in a scatter pattern often referred to as *chan*. Fine gold thread wrapped around a wooden peg (*fatila*) is twisted each time a couched stitch is put in to lay it on the ground fabric (white silk is used for silver thread and yellow for gold) in a technique known as *marorhi*. *Marorhi* work was characteristic of Sindh, and beautiful examples are still to be seen on the silk *kurtas* and *abas* of Memon communities in Karachi who have close links with Kutch and Gujarat (fig. 75).

TOP LEFT 68 Woman's shoes (*tauranwari jooti*), Vicholo, central Sindh, mid 20th century (Sindh Provincial Museum, Hyderabad). Calf leather with silk tufts. L. 25 cm, W. 14 cm.

ABOVE 69 Woman's shoes (*jooti*), Kandhkot, Jacobabad, 1994 (collection N. Askari). Leather embroidered with silk, silver-wrapped thread and silk pompons. L. 29 cm, W. 9.5 cm

TOP RIGHT 70 Woman's wedding costume: divided skirt (*gharara*), tunic (*kameez*) and shawl (*dupatta*), Karachi, *ca.* 1976 (collection N. Askari). Woven silk and gold fabric, chiffon embroidered with gold-wrapped thread, sequins, applied gold ribbon (*gota*) and gold-thread fringe. *Gharara*: L. 112 cm, W. 246 cm; *kameez*: L. 80 cm, W. 39.5 cm; *dupatta*: L. 250 cm, W. 116 cm. Additional ornamentation often includes different widths and forms of flattened or twisted gold thread and beads.

RIGHT 71 Man's robe (*angrakho*), Hyderabad or Khairpur, mid 19th century (Victoria and Albert Museum 05648 IS). Silk woven with gold-wrapped thread, lined and quilted, woven gold-thread ribbon and buttons, woven red, yellow and blue silk edging and ties. L. 104 cm, W. across sleeves 114 cm.

72 Man's waistcoat (*sadri*). Formerly worn at the court of Mir Muhammad Naseer Khan, Hyderabad, probably early 19th century (private collection). Felted wool embroidered with silk and gold-wrapped thread, applied silk and gold-thread ribbon, metal spangles and gold braid. L. 55 cm, W. 51 cm.

ABOVE Back of fig. 72

BELOW 73 Book cover, probably Karachi, mid 19th century (Victoria and Albert Museum 4078 IS). Wool embroidered with silk and metal thread. L. 47.5 cm, W. 35.5 cm. Such embroidery continues to be popular on a variety of fabrics for ceremonial use.

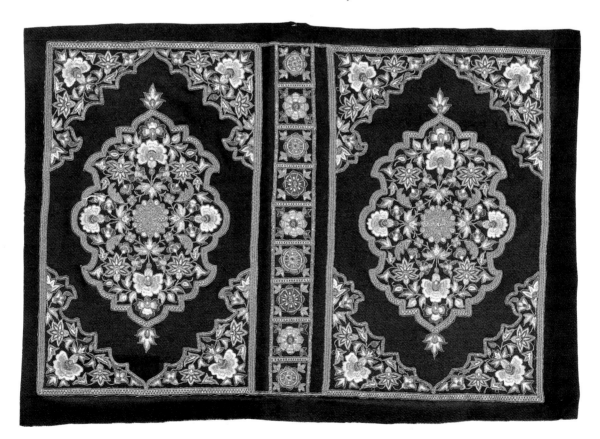

74 Two ceremonial caps, probably Zoroastrian, Karachi, early 20th century (collection Banto Kazmi). Velvet decorated with *zardozi* work, gold-wrapped thread, finely twisted gold wire (*naqshi*) and sequins. Left: diam. 16 cm, H. 10.5 cm; right: diam. 15 cm, H. 6.5 cm.

76 Embroidered panel, probably Karachi, mid 19th century (Victoria and Albert Museum 4539 IS). Wool with silk embroidery. L. 37 cm, W. 37 cm. It may have been commissioned as a cushion cover. The composition suggests that it may have been intended for the European market.

75 Woman's tunic (*aba*), Memon community, Karachi, late 19th to early 20th century (collection F. Samee). Tie-dyed silk, embroidered with couched gold thread (*marorhi*). L. 118 cm, W. across sleeves 105 cm.

Quilted Textiles Rallis (quilts) are made and used all over Sindh. *R*allis (from *ralanna* 'to mix or link') provide a practical form of reusing cloth by joining it to another. Often made up of layers of old cloth, a structure born out of necessity, *rallis* are used as carrying cloths, saddle-cloths, dowry bags, cradles, coverlets and, when suitably embellished, as canopies.

The two most common techniques are appliqué (*tukwari*) and patchwork (*chutkinwari*). Appliqué quilts are adorned with white or coloured cut-outs sewn on to a background fabric. In patchwork quilts, cut-outs conform to geometric shapes that are attached and fitted to each other to form an overall pattern. Additional embellishments in the *tukwari* style often include ornamental needlework on the edges of the appliqué, embroidered motifs, mirrors, tassels, cowrie shells, beads and sequins. *R*allis are an essential feature of rural hospitality and *ralli*-making today is a popular social custom among Sindh's rural communities, very rarely seen as a solitary domestic pursuit. The making of a dowry quilt (*athkundi*) in particular is a community affair: after the all important upper layer (*mathay jo parh*) has been prepared, each member of

77 A patchwork quilt (*chutkinwari ralli*), on a rooftop string bed (*charpai*), Thatta, 1994

78 Jokhia Baloch women working on a *ralli* near Amri, Dadu, 1995

the group having worked on the shape and laying of the cut-outs, the *ralli vijhannu* or ritual layering of the *ralli* commences with friends and relatives being invited to sing, stitch and contribute old or new fabric, fragrant herbs, cloves and dried cardamom to attach and make up the intervening layers. The lowermost layer (*hethan jo parh*) of the *ralli* usually consists of a sheet of dark fabric or an old *ajrak*. A simple running stitch or *kunh* anchors the various layers together and marks the finale of the ritual. Members of the bride's family later complete the *ralli* by creating patterns with the *kunh* (see fig. 78).

Ralli colours and styles vary slightly in the different areas of Sindh. In the delta around Thatta and Badin,

Jat nomadic and farming groups tend to leave unadorned spaces in the centres of their *rallis* with a broad border of red-, black- and white-coloured patchwork all around. The centre field often consists of a panel of tie-dyed or old re-dyed cloth. Groups in the central plains around Hyderabad, Matiari, Hala and Nawabshah tend to favour a dramatic chequerboard design of squares or compartments containing elaborate floral appliqués (*chaugulo*, *athgulo* and *naugulo*), with a border resembling a paper chain cut-out, framed by serrated bands of appliqué. Innovative techniques have also led to more varied designs using multicoloured squares and highlights for the appliqué patterns and the ground fabric. The appliqué shapes appear to draw on patterns seen on fifteenth- to nineteenth-century tombs at Chaukundi in the Thatta district.

The *rallis* of the Nara Valley on the eastern aspect of the central plains, especially the areas around Sanghar, Samaro and Umarkot, are well known for their range of intricate appliqué work (*zanjeeri*, *chand taranwari*, *popati* and *tamki*) together with vibrant combinations of colours in patchwork (fig. 82).

The Baluch groups from the west and the Mahars who have settled in the northern plains of Sindh near Ghotki, Mirpur Mathelo and Sukkur employ sophisticated combinations of both the appliqué and patchwork techniques. The appliqué forms are very finely cut, their cusped edges often only a few millimetres in width, and stitched on to squares that alternate with other patchwork squares. All the squares with their surrounding frames are smaller in size than those of *rallis* of the central plains and the colours are generally restricted to red, yellow, blue and white. Black and white is also a popular colour combination. This *ralli* tradition extends northwards along a belt of the Cholistan Desert in southern Punjab as far north as Bahawalpur (see fig. 79).

In the Tharparkar desert and in many areas of Badin, *rallis* are often made entirely in a patchwork of coloured bands or squares with an attractive *kanbiri* anchor stitch, a back stitch employed in concentric polyhedron shapes that create a compelling illusion of line and form (fig. 81). *Kanbiri rallis* were traditionally presented to *mursheds* or spiritual guides by their devotees, but today they have become dowry gifts

79 Quilt (*ralli*), Mahar group, Mirpur Mathelo, Sukkur, mid 20th century (private collection). Cotton, quilted and appliqué. L. 185 cm, W. 114 cm.

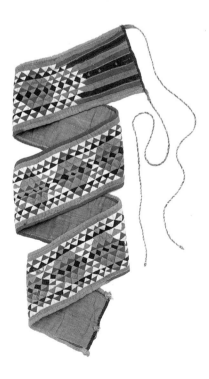

80 Quilted swaddling band (*thanjanh*), Tando Jan Mohammed, Mirpurkhas, mid 20th century (collection N. Askari). Quilted and appliqué cotton. L. 154 cm, W. 14 cm.

81 Quilted bag (*kanbiri bhujki*), Bulrhi Shah Karim, Thatta, early 20th century (collection N. Askari; gift of Syed Imdad Karimi Shah). Cotton, quilted with silk stitching and tassels. L. 38 cm, W. 43 cm. Quilted bags and purses such as these with a traditional *kanbiri* stitch were used by the Syeds (direct descendants of the Prophet Muhammad) or were presented to spiritual guides (*pirs*) and mentors (*mursheds*) by their protégés as tributes, but are now being made as dowry gifts.

82 Quilt (*ralli*), Sanghar, Vicholo, inscribed with the maker's name *Haji Mohammed Musa Wasan*, early 20th century (Justice Feroze Nana Collection, Sindh Provincial Museum, Hyderabad). Quilted cotton with appliqué cut-outs, mirrors and tassels. L. 214 cm, W. 114 cm.

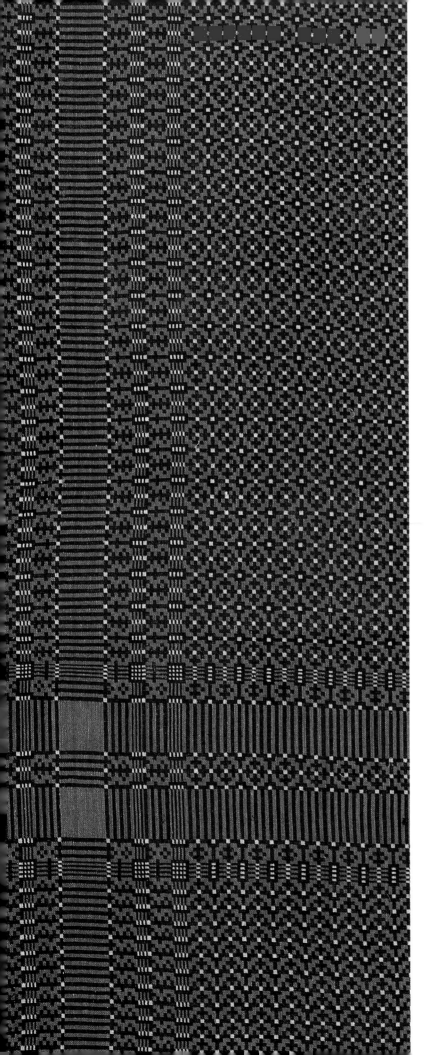

and lesser versions are used by *faqirs* and mendicants, who can also be seen carrying wraps, bags and purses made in the same technique and adorned with tassels and buttons or edged in a couched-black cotton stitch. A different version of the *kanbiri ralli* is the *jogi ralli* used by snake-charmers as wraps and spreads. The ground fabric may be laid out in a similar fashion to the *kanbiri* or in bands to form sequential rectangles but the stitches are a combination of the cretan, cross, double-running and back varieties. *Rallis* can be seen in the courtyards of shrines (*dargahs*) throughout Sindh today as devotees and their families camp out in the open to participate in anniversary (*urs*) celebrations of Sufi poets and saints revered for their humanist preaching of Islam.

In towns such as Karachi, Hyderabad, Hala, Thatta, Nagarparkar and Jacobabad commercially produced *rallis* in cottage industry workshops are beginning to find usage as soft furnishings. Enormous colourful compositions are popular as tents and canopies (*shamianas*) or movable cloth panels (*qanats*) at public gatherings, weddings and festivals.

Cotton-Weaving When Alexander the Great arrived in the Indus Valley (*ca.* 325 BC) the Greek soldiers saw people wearing clothes made from "tree wool" or "wool produced in nuts".[12] Cotton has always been a staple crop of Sindh. It is utilized in a vast range of products, from the coarse packing fabric, *dangari*, to richly woven and striped cloth, popularized by the Talpur Mirs of Khairpur, Mirpurkhas and Hyderabad in the latter part of the eighteenth century. Before the import of machine-made goods from Britain and Europe in the mid nineteenth century, small-scale cottage industries in Gambat, Hala, Nasarpur, Thatta and Karachi were well known for their hand-looms, producing cotton *soosi* trouser material, *khes* for bedcovers, *lungis* or large scarves used as male turbans and waistbands, *jori* or coarse cloth for towels, and *agath* used as drawstrings for trousers (*shalwar*).[13]

Gambat and Kandiaro in northern Sindh, and Nasarpur and Sehwan in central Sindh, continue to

83 Detail of a length of woven cotton (*khes*) in a four-corner weave pattern (*nasbi chautak*), Nasurpur or Gambat, mid 19th century (Victoria and Albert Museum 8581 IS).
L. 272 cm, W. 74 cm.

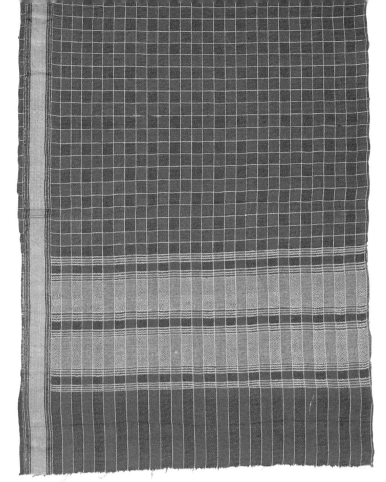

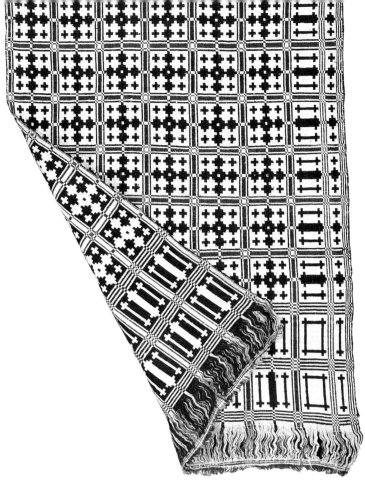

84 Detail of length of woven silk and cotton (*khes*), Gambat or Khairpur, Siro, *ca*. 1867 (Victoria and Albert Museum 5193 IS). L. 560 cm, W. 73 cm. Acquired from the Exposition Universelle in Paris in 1867.

85 Length of woven cotton (*khes*), Karachi jail, *ca*. 1880 (Victoria and Albert Museum IS 210-1883). L. 466 cm, W. 61 cm.

86 Detail of length of woven cotton (*khes*), Nasarpur, Hyderabad, mid 19th century (Victoria and Albert Museum 5142 IS). L. 265 cm, W. 74 cm.

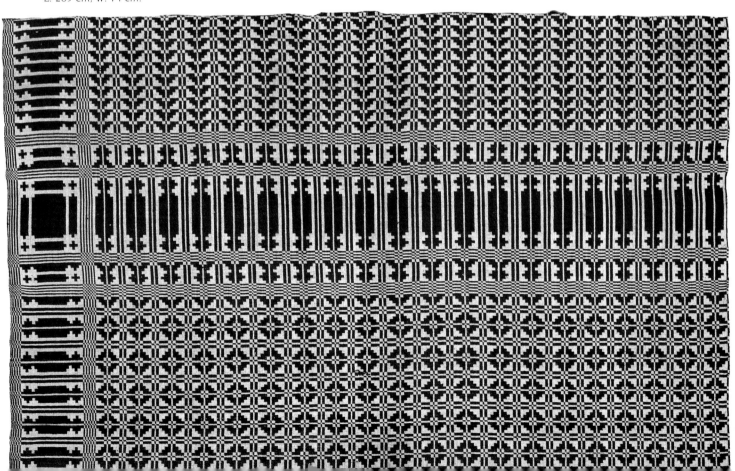

87 Man's hats (*topi*), probably Hyderabad, Vicholo, mid 19th century (Victoria and Albert Museum 5770 IS and 5769 IS). Woven silk and gold fabric with velvet. Left: H. 10 cm, diam. 27cm; right: H. 10.5 cm, diam. 26.5 cm. Hats such as these were worn at the courts of the Talpur Mirs (1783–1843) in Hyderabad, Khairpur and Mirpurkhas.

88 Painting of the Talpur Mirs, Mir's Palace, Gidu, Hyderabad, 1996. Note the colourful *lungis* around their waists and hats similar to those in fig. 87.

produce fine-quality cotton and silk *khes* today. This is a densely woven cotton or silk-and-cotton fabric most often used as a spread or coverlet. It continues to be woven in traditional geometric patterns on a pit-loom using a twill or double-weave technique. The main field is filled with a small repeating pattern, usually a diamond, a triangle or a polyhedron enclosed within a square. The end borders are wide and combine a number of narrow and broad stripes in complex permutations of the forms seen in the field. K*hes* are generally woven in sets of four pairs end to end, cut and then stitched together to produce the requisite width. A *khes* with two panels joined measures about 2 m in length and 1.5 m in width. The most popular colours are deep yellow, red, black, blue and green (white being regarded as neutral). Individual names are derived from the weaves or colour combinations used, such as *pabaro* ('lotus'), *billi butho* ('cat's face'), *baaglo* ('stork'), *tikaygul* ('dot and flower'), *kuthay paer* ('dog's paw') or *panj gulo* ('five flowers'). The number of warp threads also help to determine the density and hence the quality of the *khes*: these range from 2400 to 4800 threads per piece, the finest quality being described as *bulbul chashm* ('nightingale eyes'), using five colours in the weft and up to 4800 threads in the warp. K*hes* from areas in the north of Sindh generally use bold two- (or a maximum of three-) colour patterns (fig. 84), while those around Hyderabad (figs. 83, 86) use a number of colours in both silk and cotton thread along the

ABOVE 90 Woven silk drawstring (*agath*), probably Thatta, Larh, mid 19th century (Victoria and Albert Museum 05451a IS).

LEFT 89 Length of woven silk and gold-wrapped thread, Hala or Nasarpur, Hyderabad, Vicholo, *ca.* 1867 (Victoria and Albert Museum 0630 IS). Solid stripes alternating with toothed stripes using silver-wrapped thread (*taar waro mothro* weave). L. 138 cm, W. 79 cm.

91 Length of woven silk (*lungi*), Thatta, Larh, *ca*. mid 19th century (Sindh Provincial Museum, Hyderabad). L. 248 cm, W. 135 cm.

borders and as highlights in the field pattern. Traditionally, women would arrange and fasten the warp threads but men are now responsible for this task and for the entire weaving process. As *khes* are labour intensive and expensive to produce, finer weaves in Gambat are made only as private commissions.

Khadar, formerly known as *khadi*, though now used to refer to all woven cloth from Sindh apart from *soosi*, is a textured cotton cloth woven by hand and machine throughout Pakistan. It is commonly used for both men and women's *shalwar kameez*, and in varying densities for more utilitarian purposes.

Silk-Weaving A typical cotton or silk-and-cotton combined fabric, referred to as *soosi*, was traditionally used for trouser (*shalwar*) material by both men and women all over Sindh. It is a finely woven striped cloth in which the warp threads conform to the colours of the stripes, often multicoloured, while the weft threads are made up of a single colour only. Like the *khes* it is woven on a pit-loom, but a large number of power-looms are currently employed in Nasarpur, Khohra, Gambat, Hala and Khairpur. Weaves were originally restricted to specific colours but this discipline has largely disappeared and a large number of colours and patterns are being used together. *Garbi* and *ailacho* are terms used to differentiate *soosi* woven entirely from silk. *Mothro* describes a type of weave in which individual solid coloured stripes are edged with fine black-and-white toothed lines. When a silver or gold thread is included in this pattern it is referred to as *chumki* or *taar waro mothro* (see fig. 89). Other *mothro* combinations include H*alaki mothro*, M*atiari mothro*, *gharo mothro* (red), *bito sao mothro* (double green) and *zanjeer mothro* (linked-chain pattern). The most popular traditional weaves are the *sao popat* ('green butterfly'), *mor khumb sao* ('green peacock feather'), *karo kukar akh* ('black chicken eyes') and *khoonbi wal* ('red vine'). An average *soosi shalwar* can use from five to twenty metres of cloth; synthetic yarns and imported dyes are now popularly used in its manufacture and it is no longer worn by men in Sindh.

Lungis are silk turbans or sashes that were traditionally worn by Sindhi men. Postans, writing in 1840, reports "among the goods brought to Shikarpur by

92 Length of woven silk and gold-wrapped thread (*lungi*), probably Thatta, Larh, *ca.* 1855 (Victoria and Albert Museum 0556 IS). L. 370 cm, W. 71 cm. This magnificent lungi shows a variety in design and width of toothed stripes with solid coloured red, yellow and pink bands.

caravans from Kandahar, raw silk of six distinct qualities from Bokhara, Herat and Yezd ...".[14] Silk was being spun and dyed in Shikarpur before being sent as far afield as Sehwan and Thatta to be woven.

Early travellers in Sindh all comment on the sumptuous turbans, scarves and sashes that were patronized by the Talpur Mirs who ruled Sindh from 1783 until the British annexation in 1843 (see figs. 88, 91, 92). At the time, silk was woven in Sukkur, Rohri, Khairpur, Ranipur, Thatta and Hyderabad using natural dyes like indigo, madder, saffron, safflower, cochineal and *musagh* (a dye obtained from walnuts),[15] and in addition to Iran it was also being imported from Bombay, Muscat and China. *Lungis* became a hallmark of the Talpurs. "These magnificent cloths which the Talpur chieftains often unrolled from their waists and handed with a royal gesture to visiting ambassadors as a token of the highest favour they could bestow" began to decline in popularity and use

from the end of their rule.[16] As turbans, *lungis* were tied without a *kulah* or supporting hat. A number of weaves acquired poetic names such as *dilpasand* ('heart's desire'), *lehrdar* ('waves') and *nangwal* ('studded with gems').

Although *lungis* are not considered part of a man's dress accessories today, beautiful silk and cotton *lungis* are still woven in Hala, Gambat, Khairpur and Shikarpur. They continue to be used as wedding gifts, tributes at funerals and as formal presentations to visitors. For a Sindhi there can be no greater accolade than the gift of a well made *lungi*.

In urban centres such as Karachi, Hyderabad, Hala and Khairpur, silks, silk blends using synthetic yarns and fine *jamayvaar* brocades for saris, *kurtas*, *shalwars* and *dupattas* and the ceremonial long divided skirts, *gharara*, are being woven as there is an ever increasing demand for their use at social occasions and ceremonies.

93 Woven storage bag (*kothro*), Mahar group, Kunion Ganwhar, Badin, early 20th century (collection N. Askari). Sheep's wool and cotton. L. 91 cm, W. 50 cm.

Woollen Textiles Sindhi carpets are of two kinds, cotton *daris* and woollen *farasis* (derived from the Persian word *farsh*, 'floor'). The flat-woven cotton *daris* are used as floor-coverings and are produced in a variety of colours and qualities. The earliest recorded *daris* had been made in jails in Khairpur, Hyderabad and Karachi.

Woollen *farasis* and storage bags are woven by settlers of Baluch origin and the Mahars in villages in Kohistan, Guni, Kunion Ganwhar and Golarchi in Badin, around Ghotki in Sukkur and in Tharparkar (see fig. 5, p. 11). Patterns generally consist of coloured bands with fine, alternating geometric patterns. The quality and texture vary greatly according to the wool used for the weft. As dyed and undyed camel, goat and sheep's wool are commonly used, the colours range from white, grey and black to shades of brown. Madder and indigo were traditionally used in the weft and consisted of a deep red and blue with green highlights (see fig. 93). More recent combinations include the same colours using synthetic dyes with highlights in red, orange and silver thread being favoured. The warp continues to be made up of white cotton threads spun locally or purchased in neighbouring towns. The ends of the larger floor rugs, once the weaving is complete, are made into tiny plaits, with tassels added as a finishing touch.

Finely woven cotton *farasis* are used to sleep on and as prayer mats. A coarser version, woven entirely from camel or goat's hair (see fig. 95), called *khirir*,[17] is found in villages in Kohistan and Badin and is used for saddle bags (*khurzeen*), nosebags (*tobro*) and for storing grain (*boro*). Women are usually responsible for weaving *farasis* and work in pairs on very simple ground-looms, using a floating weft technique. The looms are usually set up in shaded areas of the *otaro* or courtyard and covered when not in use, as women return to the task of weaving when they can make time from their household chores.

Beautiful woollen shawls or wraps for men, called *khatho*, are also woven in Tharparkar. *Khatho* are usually worn by Meghwar and Rabari men and woven in halves. These are traditionally white, brown or black and woven from undyed wool, although brightly dyed versions in orange appear to be very popular. They often have plain fields with coloured woven borders,

or additional small borders using coloured wools in a supplementary weft technique (fig. 94). Lightweight ceremonial woollen shawls (often using synthetic yarn), called *loee*, are worn by women and these have auspicious woven patterns of temples and mounds or embroidery on them. One of the beneficial effects of mass tourism for neighbouring Rajasthan is that *khatha* are now being made there in copious numbers on power-looms to cater to a commercial demand. While hand-looms continue to be the norm in Tharparkar, inevitably cheaper Rajasthani pieces are brought across the border.

A number of animal trappings are still woven in Tharparkar and Badin (see fig. 65). Ceremonial camel girths (*jhul*), bullock and donkey trappings are made from a variety of wools using ply-split braiding techniques. Felt (*tal*) is made in Badin and parts of the Dadu district for use in animal saddles and as floor rugs and bedding.

94 A vendor of woollen wraps (*khatho*), Mithi, Tharparkar, 1995

95 Men weaving a rug (*khirir*) from goat's hair on a simple ground-loom, near Mehar, Dadu, 1994

Block-Printing "Thatta chintzes were considered to be far superior in texture and pattern to those made in most other parts of India."[18] There are ancient and diverse traditions of dyeing and printing cloth all over Sindh, from the single coloured red *laso* or *hik rango* to the complex resist- and mordant-dyed *ajrak*. Block-printing (*chur*) uses specially carved blocks of wood (*por*) sequentially dipped in dyes and stamped on cloth. Sheets, coverlets, wall-hangings, *qanats* (cloths used for screening off areas), *dastarkhans* (tablecloths), shouldercloths, wraps of all sizes and women's costume are all *chur*-printed in a variety of patterns and colours (see fig. 96). The *kambo* is a simple but striking muslin, block-printed shawl with a latticed floral pattern especially used by Soomrah brides throughout Sindh. The *por* have individual names depending on the design carved into them (*jholo, vat, booto, guldasto, chaman* and *val*) or their shape (*pato, chaukri, nimuri* and *ambri*). In a number of urban centres, block-printing is done on cotton, silk and a variety of synthetic fabrics, silver and gold printing being a popular substitute for expensive woven brocades. Although contemporary dyers use a range of chemical compounds they continue to adhere to traditional methods of preparing and finishing the cloth.

As mordant-dyeing was known in the Indus Valley as early as 1500 BC we can only speculate on how this process may have evolved into the complex patterns of the seventeenth century. Mordants are naturally occurring substances or chemicals that are added to dye baths in order to fix the dye by forming an insoluble compound with it. Mordant-dyeing in red is the most intricate dye process and historically a spectrum of shades in red has been achieved using madder (*Rubia tinctorum*) or *al* (genus *Morinda*) in conjunction with an alum mordant which produces a red or brick red, or an iron mordant for darker reds; but today a range of aniline compounds are in use. Preparation of the cloth with soaps, oils and an astringent prior to applying the mordant is crucial as this prevents the mordant from crystallizing and helps it to bind the dye to the fibres of the cloth.

Mordant-dyeing is carried out in Badin, Tharparkar and the Sanghar districts, the simplest patterns being dyed red and black using alum and iron mordants with the occasional use of indigo. Gathered skirts or *parha* in Tharparkar are generally printed in small, repeating floral patterns, alternating with bands enclosing a tendril, birds or dots. Depending on the motif, patterns are referred to as *pungriyo, gulbadan, boriai, ambar* or *meena kari*. Dyers are traditionally known as *khatris* or *katis* and dyeing with indigo is generally carried on by artisans referred to as *nirolis* in the north and *nirotis* in the south. Resist-dyed shoulder wraps called *maleers* are generally worn by women but are also embroidered for use by by Meghwar bridegrooms (see fig. 26). Similar mordant-dyed red-and-black veils with a repeating floral or geometric pattern and multiple narrow borders (*jimmi*) are worn by women and resemble one-sided *ajraks* in their technique of production.

Tie-Dyeing Oral traditions relate that tie-dyeing techniques (*bandhani*) travelled from the eastern areas of Sindh to Kutch and Gujarat. *Bandhani* is a style of patterning cloth by tying or knotting specific areas to protect them from the dye (*bandhana* is 'to tie'). The cloth is prepared with soap and treated with oil and an alum mixture before it is tied. *Bandhani* patterns vary in intricacy from a single dot to a combination of borders and medallions. The prepared cloth is first marked out with a dotted pattern; it is folded into four, steamed and then pressed over a board embedded with nails to obtain an imprint, or printed with a charcoal and water mix. It is then sent to a *bandhnari* or knotter, usually a woman, who picks up a tiny piece of cloth from each marked dot and ties it in a knot (*bindi*) with a piece of waxed string. When tying has been completed the cloth is taken over by a dyer (*khatri*) who dips it into the dye required for the ground colour. After drying, the knots are unfastened, the parts tied having resisted the dye to form white circles (see fig. 97). This is the simplest *chundari* (or *chunari*) pattern. In more complex designs such as the flower garden (*phulvadi*), knotting further areas and dyeing are repeated for each colour. Umarkot, Chachro, Diplo, Mithi and Ghulam Nabi Shah in Tharparkar and Tando Mohammed Khan, Badin and Khipro in Sanghar are well known for their tie-dyed cottons. The urban centres of Karachi and Hyderabad specialize in elaborate tie-dyed silks. Numerous references to tie-dyed cloth as symbols of fidelity are found in Sindhi folk poetry, for example in Shah Abdul Latif's rendition of the tale of Umar and Marvi:

Threads around my wrist Maru tied, of gold,
Beautiful gold, they are for me,
Umar, do not offer silks to a rustic maiden –
For they leave me cold
Much dearer do I hold my worn *bandhani*.

Ajrak Of all the techniques used for the adornment of cloth in Sindh, the mordant-dyeing and resist-printing of cotton *ajrak* is perhaps the best known. Although historical records for the production of *ajrak* are sparse, we have evidence of a medieval trade in similarly printed cotton textiles from the north-west of India to the Mediterranean along the trade routes of the Indian Ocean. A corpus of these block-printed textiles (employing a resist or a mordant or often both) found at Fostat outside Cairo in the late nineteenth century provides us with the earliest examples of textiles from the Indian subcontinent. The correspondence of technique and pattern between these somewhat coarse fragments and those of the *ajrak* repertoire in Sindh, however, remains to be explored more thoroughly.

An *ajrak* is a rectangular cotton textile traditionally used by men in Sindh as a shawl, shoulder cloth or turban, but it also serves a number of useful functions as a wrap, a carrying cloth, a hammock or a spread. Aitken mentions a number of well known *ajrak* centres along the Indus, among them Karachi, Thatta, Jerruck and Hyderabad.[19] The best known areas for traditional *ajraks* today are Malook Shah, Tando Mohammed Khan, Matiari, Hala, Badin, Matli, Seykhat, Kheybar and Bhit Shah.

The term *ajrak* may have evolved from *azrak*, Arabic for blue. The colours of the traditional *ajrak* are shades of blue and red (indigo and madder being the principal dyes), with shapes of the white background fabric showing through. *Ajrak* blocks fall into two

96 Length of printed cotton, Hala, Hyderabad, Vicholo, mid 20th century (collection N. Askari). It shows the *nimuri* pattern, derived from the fruit of the *neem* tree (*Azadricta indica*).

97 Tie-dyed cotton shawl (*bandhani*), made by Gopal Das, Hathungo, Khipro, Sanghar, *ca.* 1978 (collection N. Askari)

broad categories: squares and rectangles.[20] Those with square outlines are the *kharek* ('date'), *mor* ('peacock'), *jalayb* ('a sweetmeat'), *chakki* ('mortar'), *badaam* ('almond'), *ishq pech* ('knots of love'), *chalo* ('ring') and *ghaleecho* ('floor-covering'). These are all constructed by intersecting horizontal, vertical and diagonal lines around a fixed central point. Rectangular blocks tend to have vegetative or undulating motifs such as the *wal* ('vine') and the *kakkar* ('cloud').

The *ajrak* is traditionally printed on both sides (*bepassi*), a less elaborate form being printed on one side only (*hik passi*), and has bands or rectangular frames making up its borders, the most intricate pattern of which is the *hashe ji ajrak* or triple border. The end borders are referred to as the *paland* and invariably consist of two borders of medallions and fluted arches (*mihrabs*) on short pillars, separated by a triple white stripe or *naro*. The side borders, however, vary in number and pattern, each with its own *wat* or subsidiary borders. The *wat* usually contain small, stylized flowers on a continuous vine with leaves, and the simpler *ajrak* may sometimes have only a single *wat* along its sides (see figs. 101, 102). Ajraks are generally distinguished by the pattern on the central field and the configuration of the side borders.

Ajrak-making is a complex process involving the skilful use of mordants and resists to dye areas of fabric selectively. Cotton cloth is generally purchased locally and cut into five-metre lengths for a pair of *ajraks*. Each piece is prepared by repeated washing (*khumbh*), oiling (*sajj*) and immersion in a solution of ground tamarisk seeds, molasses, oil and water (*kasai*) to help soften it and rid it of starch. Printing is then carried out with specially prepared wooden blocks (*por*) in three stages: *asul*, in which a resist is first stamped to mark the white outlines and flowers of the *ajrak* pattern; *kot*, using a mordant for areas that will turn black on dyeing; and *khaar*, when a resist and mordant mix is applied to all the areas not to be dyed blue. The cloth, while still wet, is sprinkled with powdered cow dung or ground rice bran on both sides to fix the resists, and it is then hung up to dry.

Dyeing commences with the fabric being finely pleated and immersed in a cold indigo bath (*kun jo marhalo*). It is dried and then thoroughly washed in water until the areas printed with the mordant for red

98 Man wearing an *ajrak* wrap over an embroidered Sindhi cap (*topi*), Thatta, 1995

appear grey and those resisted to stay white are washed clean. Alizarine (red) dyeing follows in a vat close to boiling for a period of two hours. By careful dipping, soaking and heating, together with the judicious addition of ground acacia seeds, a rich red tone is achieved (the lines stamped in the *asul* stage remain undyed and the *kot* areas turn black). The cloth is then cooled and soaked in a mixture of camel dung and water (*gissi*), wrung and kept aside overnight. An intensive phase of soaking in water and beating the *ajraks* on stone slabs (*tapai*) ensues before they are spread in the sun on the river banks. As the *ajraks* begin to dry the dyer continues to sprinkle water over them and their colours begin to darken (see fig. 100). *Tapai* continues, each surface of the *ajrak* being dealt with separately, until the dryer is satisfied that all excess dye has been removed and the white areas are crisp in form. Master craftsmen pre-

99 *Ajrak* block-printing, Matiari, Hyderabad, 1996

100 Sprinkling water on *ajraks* during the *tapai* stage of preparation, on the banks of the Indus, near Khebar, Hyderabad, 1996

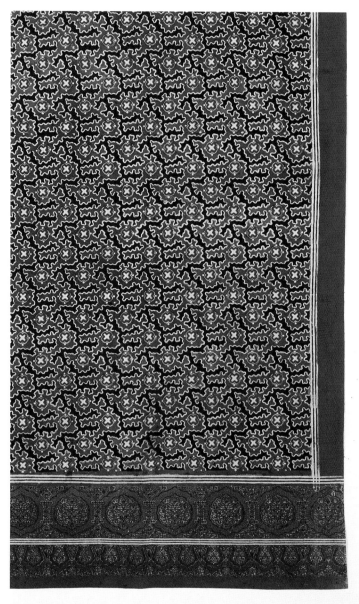

101 *Ajrak* with a cloud (*kakkar*) pattern, Tando Mohammed Khan, Hyderabad, Vicholo, *ca.* 1971 (private collection). L. 252 cm, W. 182 cm.

fer to soak their *ajraks* in the river for a protracted period; this is a crucial determinant of the final colour of red achieved: exposure to the sun, the hardness of the water and whether it is running or stagnant are all important considerations. *Ajraks* from Larh are a brighter red than those of Vicholo. The final stage in dyeing is now performed by printing a resist on all the areas except those that have already been dyed blue, following the very first stage of indigo dyeing. The second indigo dyeing is referred to as the *meena* stage (literally 'enamelling') and is designed to refine and darken the blue colour obtained earlier.

102 *Ajrak* panel, probably Thatta, Larh, mid 19th century (Victoria and Albert Museum 5448b IS)

103 Quilt (*ralli*) lined with one-sided (*hik passi*) *ajrak*, used at the shrine of the Sufi poet and philosopher Shah Abdul Latif (1689–1752), Bhit Shah, Hyderabad, *ca*. late 19th century (courtesy Faqir Allah Dino Tamarani, custodian of the shrine of Shah Abdul Latif at Bhit Shah). L. 208 cm, W. 120 cm. *Ajraks* are traditionally printed on both sides of the cloth, but the lining of this quilt is printed on one side only. It has been suggested that this may have been an earlier stage in the evolution of *ajrak*-printing.

A F G H A N I S T A N

• Kandahar

NWF

Zhob •

Sulaiman Range

• Chaman

• Pishin

■ Quetta

• Loralai

• Mach

Bibi Nani

Barkhan •

Mastung •

Bolan Pass

Dadhar • Sibi •

• Nushki

B A L U C H I S T A N

Chagai Hills

• Chagai

Mehgarh
(Archaeological
Excavations)

Kachhi

• Lahri

Dera Bugti •

PUNJ

• Dalbandin

Kalat •

Desert

• Kharan

Harboi Hills

Central Brahui Range

Temple Dera
(Dera Murad Jamali)

Sui •

Nasirabad •

Khanpur •   • Jacobabad

Khuzdar •

Siahan Range

Central Makran Range

• Nal

Kirthar Range

Indus

Wad •

S I N D H

I R A N

• Panjgur

Mashkai

Nal

Arra

Mor Range

Saruna

• Mand

Turbat • Kech Valley

Makran Coastal Range

Haibo

• Bela

Sonmiani •

Dasht

Hingol

Hab

Jiwani •

• Gwadar

• Pasni

• Ormara

■ Karachi

Sonmiani Bay

A r a b i a n   S e a

0   50   100   miles   150

0   50   100   150   kms

Baluchistan

Extending in arid plains and divided by impenetrable mountain ranges, Baluchistan is the largest but most sparsely populated province of Pakistan. On its western border it adjoins Iran and Afghanistan, with both of which it has strong historical and cultural links. Baluchistan is largely inhabited by nomadic and semi-nomadic groups whose culture and traditions are distinct from those of the settled and cultivated areas in the rest of Pakistan. Bray tells us, "Of ancient Baluchistan strangely little is known, yet it lies on one of the great highways trodden by the many conquerors of India. Achaemenian, Macedonian, Arab, Ghaznavid, Moghul, Afsharid and Durrani have sojourned in it and after a brief sojourn passed on, leaving scarce a trace behind."[1] Although records of their origins are scanty, the indigenous inhabitants of Baluchistan at the time of the Arab invasion in the eighth century appear to have been the Meds, Afghans and Jats.[2] The principal ethnic groups today are the Baluch, the Brahvi, the Pathans and the Makranis, all of whom are organized into numerous tribes with subgroups. The Baluch, consisting of the Marris, Bugtis, Buledis, Magsis, Rinds, Dombkis, Lagharis, Lasharis, Jatois, Jamalis, Umranis, Mazaris, Karmatis, Korais and Burdis, live in the eastern

Sulaiman range and parts of the central Kachhi plain. The Brahvis, who include the Brohis, Raisanis, Shahwanis, Bangulzai, Kurds, Lehris, Zehris, Mengals, Bizenjos and Marwaris, frequent the mountain ranges and plains that fan out from the capital Quetta down to Las Bela. The Pathans are generally to be found in the north of the province, continuing across the Sulaiman range and its extension into the North-West Frontier. Following the Soviet invasion of Afghanistan in 1979 large numbers of refugees have settled in north Baluchistan and the adjoining belt of the North-West Frontier Province. The Makran coast at the Arabian Sea, which marks Baluchistan's southern limit, is occupied by the Makrani peoples and the Jats (Lasis) who have ancient maritime links with Muscat, Oman, the Horn of Africa and, through the Persian Gulf, with Europe.

Women's garments all over Baluchistan consist of an ankle-length, loose-fitting, long-sleeved dress (*pashk*) over gathered trousers (*shalwar*) and a large shawl (*chadar*). The traditional Baluch male costume consisted of coarse white or indigo cotton trousers worn with a long shirt or smock (*jama*) reaching to just below the knees and buttoned over the right shoulder. This was worn under a robe-like garment, also of

104 Bugti tribesman sporting traditional turban (*pag*), overcoat (*kaba*) and woollen shawl (*sal*), Dera Bugti, 1997

105 Baluch girl outside her house, near Mand, Makran, 1994

106 Makrani girl wearing a traditional Makrani dress (*pashk*) and trousers (*shalwar*), Pidarak, Makran, 1994

107 A shepherd and his flock outside Sibi, Kach, 1996

108 Nomads travelling along the Makran coast with all their belongings, Sonmiani, 1996. Mats made from dwarf palm (*peesh*) have felts thrown over them.

109 Woman's dress (*pashk*), from Nal or Khuzdar, late 19th- or early 20th century (Victoria and Albert Museum IS 14-1971). Silk with silk and gold-thread embroidery, mirrors, woven gold-thread ribbon, silk and gold-thread braid and tassels.
L. 126 cm,
W. 50 cm.

This exceptionally fine *pashk*, with contrasting silk gussets under the arms, is embroidered in a popular *gul-o-airkash* pattern composed of finely worked geometric medallions on each shoulder extending in columns over the bosom. The sleeves are embroidered in a scattered floral motif (*buti*), with small openings to facilitate nursing.

FACING PAGE
Detail of shoulder and yoke embroidery (*jeegh*) of fig. 109

110 Woman's dress (*pashk*), probably from Kalat, late 19th to early 20th century (Victoria and Albert Museum IS 33-1969). Silk embroidered with silk thread, woven gold-thread ribbon, braid and silk tassel. L. 131 cm, W. 50 cm. The yoke is framed by columns of chevrons embroidered in a delicate satin stitch (*band zari mosum*). The embroidery along the border framing the central pocket does not conform to the overall style of embroidery and may have been a later addition.

FACING PAGE Detail of yoke of fig. 110

cotton, densely pleated at the waist and tied to one side with strings (*kurti*).[3] Today the *jama* and *kurti* have largely been replaced by the ubiquitous *kameez* or long shirt, worn with simple drawstring trousers (*shalwar*). Other important male dress accessories are the long scarf or shoulder wrap (*pushti*) and turban (*pag*) wrapped in numerous large rolls over a snugly fitting cap (*topi*). In colder weather, woollen socks, an overcoat (*kaba*) or waistcoat (*sadri*) are popular, with a woollen shawl (*saal*) occasionally tied around the waist and knees to help maintain a squatting position (*kamarzani*).

Embroidered Textiles Baluchi embroidery (*doch*) is outstanding in its intricate repeating geometric patterns and colours. The Baluchi woman's *pashk* invariably carries four panels of embroidery: a large yoke covering the chest, the sleeve cuffs and a long, narrow, rectangular pocket (*pado* or *pandohl*) that runs from the yoke to just above the hem.[4] The embroidery is often referred to as *pakka* ('firm' or 'solid'), as the ground fabric is completely covered in a reper-

toire of fine satin (*mosum*), interlacing (*chinnuka*), herringbone (*mai pusht*), chain (*kash*), blanket, square-chain, cross- and couched stitches. While the distribution of embroidery on the *pashk* remains more or less constant throughout Baluchistan, there are minor regional variations in pattern and colour. The panels may be embroidered directly on the fabric of the *pashk*, or on pieces of coarse cotton cloth called *alwan*, which are then stitched on to the *pashk* and can be reused (*tharho*).

The silk *pashk* of Brahvi groups in Kalat, Khuzdar, Nal and Kharan in central Baluchistan have a repertoire of over fifty richly embroidered patterns using floss silk in a brilliant palette of red, orange, yellow, green, white, blue and purple or black. They were worn traditionally with contrasting baggy trousers (*shalwar*) of striped silk fabric called *kanavez* and large shawls (*chadars*) with embroidered borders, but are now worn with matching *shalwar* and *chadar*.[5]

Elaborate medallions on either side of the neck may be round (*gul*) or diamond-shaped (*kundi-e-gul*) with geometric surrounds extending in arched columns over the bosom, the whole design being referred to as *gul-o-airkush* (see fig. 109 and detail). The main patterns of the yoke and its accompanying panels are distinguishable by fixed combinations of stitches that create popular forms: *murgh padak* ('chicken feet'), *kapuk-o-nal* ('pigeon's feet'), *chandan haar* ('bride's necklace'), *gul-o-riduk* ('flower beds') and *padiwal* ('flowering vine'). They may also have subsidiary patterns made up of scattered small motifs, bands or rows of chevrons surrounded by a number of framing borders. The edges of the sleeves and the neck opening are usually strengthened with a braid of silk and gold thread or tightly packed blanket stitches (*toi*) followed by a series of finely worked narrow and wide borders in a precisely defined sequence (see fig. 110 and detail). The narrow borders are generally worked using black and white threads in a couched stitch (*chamusurma*), followed by chain (*kash*) and satin stitches (*mosum*), and this sequence is repeated symmetrically in all the narrow borders as they alternate with the wide borders. The wider borders (*wath*) are embroidered in sequential combinations of interlacing, herringbone and cross stitches. No two *wath* are the same (see detail of fig. 110).

111 Woman's dress (*pashk*), probably from Quetta, west Baluchistan, late 19th to early 20th century (Victoria and Albert Museum T.251-1923). Silk with applied panels of embroidered cotton, cotton- and silk-thread embroidery, woven gold-thread ribbon and braid. L. 125 cm, W. 45 cm. This diamond repeat pattern, often referred to as *paraiz zarto*, has been modified in different ways by groups throughout Baluchistan to produce a range of related designs.

112 Embroidered saddle-cloth, probably from Nasirabad, Kachi plain, *ca*. 1900 (Victoria and Albert Museum IM 311-1927; bequeathed by Lord Curzon of Kedleston). Woollen broadcloth with silk embroidery, deer-skin appliqué and edging, silk tassels and silver ornaments. L. 120 cm, max. W. 154 cm.

113 Woman's dress (*pashk*), silk with silk embroidery, Nasirabad area, Kachi plain, south-east Baluchistan, 19th century (Victoria and Albert Museum 849-1873). L. 137 cm, W. 57 cm. The highly unusual chain-stitch technique on this *pashk* is commonly associated with embellished leather ware from this area and across the border in north Sindh. It may have been commissioned in either Shikarpur or Jacobabad. It entered the India Museum collections in 1873, but its acquisition record states that it was "taken at the capture of Ghazni" (1842).

A variety of satin stitches are worked from the reverse side of the fabric, and pleats under the armhole (*cheen*) are stitched into colourful, contrasting gussets (*bunkash*). Pashk for ceremonial wear are usually made from silk and may be embroidered with silver or gold thread (see fig. 114). Girls are encouraged to embroider as soon as they are able and to begin to prepare their bridal dowries. The interval between betrothal and marriage is usually spent in embroidering garments, shawls and wraps, and accessories for the bridegroom.

Pashk from the Makran coast employ a similar precise layout in their embroidery but a slightly different palette of colours, two shades of red (usually red and maroon), black, white, dark green and royal blue. A conspicuous border or frame (*pat daman*), made up of

114 Woman's ceremonial dress (*pashk*), probably from Kalat, early 20th century (Victoria and Albert Museum IM 65-1930). Silk embroidered with gold thread, braid and silk tassel. L. 119 cm, W. 52 cm. Elegant silk garments such as this were popular amongst women of high rank in the Khanate groups of Kharan, Kalat, Las Bela and Makran. The cuffs of the sleeves and central pocket have subtle paisley *butis* as additional accents.

115 Small embroidered tablecloth (*maiz posht*), Bugti, *ca.* 1980 (courtesy of Mrs Nilofar Huzoor Buksh Dombki, Lahri). Cotton embroidered with silk, edged with beads and tassels.

116 Woman's dress (*pashk*), probably from Chaman or Quetta, early 20th century (Victoria and Albert Museum IS 32-1969). Cotton, embroidered with silk, mirrors and silk tassels, with silk gussets. L. 131 cm, W. 46 cm. The exquisite satin-stitch embroidery on this dress reflects the influence of Kandahari traditions of embroidery from just across the border in Afghanistan. The use of a single colour makes the embroidery particularly striking against the ivory-coloured ground.

horizontal bands of coloured stitches, surrounds the central *pudo* and may extend along the seams. This framing border varies from those of Kalat and Khuzdar in the use of the *jalar* stitch, an elongated and elaborate form of the herringbone stitch (*mai pusht*). In a number of *pashk* worn today, applied narrow braids have replaced a number of the supplementary embroidered borders.[6]

Embroidery from central Baluchistan (with Sibi and the Bolan Pass at its northern extremity down to Nasirabad and the Kirthar Range on its eastern border with Sindh) tends to combine the linear layouts of traditional *pashk* embroidery with floral and geometric motifs using tiny mirrors (*shisha*). In the south and south-east, the Kach Gundava plain, lying between Kalat and the Indus, together with the areas adjoining the border with Sindh, show a remarkable crossover style of embroidery. Satin stitch is worked

117 Embroidered purses (*bushkiri*) used for storing or carrying valuables and bridal dowry gifts.

TOP Brahvi group, probably Quetta, *ca*. 1939 (Victoria and Albert Museum IM 280.1939). Cotton embroidered with silk thread, silk tufts. L. 24.5 cm, W. (with tufts) 19 cm.

MIDDLE ROW
LEFT Samalani group, Nushki, early 20th century (collection N. Askari). Silk with cotton lining, silk embroidery, silk braid and silk tassels. L. 18 cm, W. 14 cm.
MIDDLE Probably Barech group, Chagai, mid 20th century (collection N. Askari). Cotton with silk and cotton embroidery, lined with printed cotton. L. 21 cm, W. 15 cm.

RIGHT Probably Chagai group, Dalbandin, mid 20th century (collection S.J. Cohen). Cotton with silk embroidery. L. 18.5 cm, W. 13.5 cm.

BOTTOM ROW
LEFT Probably Kalat, mid 20th century (collection N. Askari). Cotton with silk embroidery, cowrie shells, glass beads, gold-wrapped thread and silk tassels. L. 30.5 cm, W. 21 cm.
MIDDLE Probably Jamali group, Mastung, mid 20th century (collection N. Askari). Cotton with silk embroidery, silk braid and glass beads. L. 22.5 cm, W. 19 cm.
RIGHT Probably Bizenjo group, Nal or Khuzdar, mid 20th century (private collection). Cotton with silk embroidery, mirrors, cowrie shells and silk tassels. L. 29 cm, W. 23 cm.

obliquely and in varying lengths, while the interlacing stitch (*chinnuka*) is superbly executed in the borders in a refined form of the better known *hurmitch* stitch, found further east in the Vicholo areas of Sindh.

Chain stitch commonly used in Baluchi leather embroidery is also used for *pashks* in the areas around Nasirabad and Khanpur (see fig. 113). These are often embroidered in Jacobabad, Sibi or its environs. Jacobabad has evolved into a major centre of Baluchi embroidery workshops, producing ornamental panels, wallets, belts, traditional purses, spreads and caps, both for local demand and for export. The traditional Baluch cap or *topi*, over which the turban is tightly rolled and wrapped, is a deeper and more intricately embroidered version of the Sindhi *topi*. It is usually made of cotton with fine silk or cotton embroidery in floral or geometric patterns, incorporating minute mirrors and the occasional use of silver- or gold-wrapped thread for more ceremonial wear (see figs. 118, 119).

Among the Baluch groups, the Bugtis in the Sibi plains with their stronghold at Dera Bugti in the Sulaiman range of mountains favour the use of white for both men and women, and women's *pashks* do not have a central pocket. The square panel over the chest is referred to as a *jeegh* and the colours used are predominantly shades of red and black with skilfully placed accents in dark green and orange. Bugti embroidery remains largely unchanged, flowers, medallions and fine repeating geometric shapes made up of blocks of laid and couched (*shahi bundh*), satin (*bagho bundh*) and hem stitches that are outlined in fine cross, stem or honeycomb filling stitches. Men's waistcoats are also elaborately embroidered, along with small purses (*bushkiri*) and larger envelope-shaped bags (*bushka*) for carrying the Quran, money, tobacco, cosmetics *etc*. The Marris combine the medallion, diamond and chevron patterns of the Bugtis with continuous zigzag forms (*rasorhi*) in their embroideries worked in a delicate satin stitch which often uses only a single thread (*yaktari mosum*).

ABOVE 121 Man's embroidered sandals (*chabav* or *chawat*), Dombki group, Lahri (private collection). Leather with silk embroidery.

LEFT ABOVE 120 Gunbelt, Dombki group, Lahri, Sibi, late 19th century (Victoria and Albert Museum 1-1900). Leather embroidered with silk, with attachments in steel and leather. L. 143 cm, W. 4.5 cm. This leather belt is embellished with characteristic Dombki embroidery in a fine chain stitch using coloured silk thread. It would have been used with a matchlock gun and has a number of attachments for this purpose: a stitched-leather priming flask for carrying fine-grained powder, an incised metal hook for attaching a gunpowder flask, a flint and steel for igniting a match, three storage pouches, and a number of decorative pendant straps.

LEFT BELOW Detail of a bullet pouch from gunbelt, fig. 120

The highlands of Baluchistan, bounded on the north by the North-West Frontier and on the west by Afghanistan, enjoy traditions of Brahvi silk embroidery in luminous colours using interlocking diamond-, cross- and V-shaped motifs influenced by decorative traditions from further west. Since the Soviet invasion of Afghanistan in 1979, large numbers of Afghans have settled around Zhob and Loralai and in the adjoining tribal belt of the NWFP. While both Pathan and Afghan women favour similar patterns with defining borders for their yokes, they tend towards vigorous colours in silk or cotton thread and large mirrors interspersed with bold blocks of *zari* (silver- and gold-wrapped thread) embroidery. Padded or quilted embroideries are important dowry gifts; designs consist of medallions in a variety of satin stitches with columns and borders of herringbone, couched and stem stitches.

Leather Embroidery Leather is embroidered throughout Baluchistan but the articles produced in Kech in Makran, Las Bela, Nasirabad and Lahri, north of the Kachi plain, are particularly well known. A hooked awl is used with fine silk thread on leather for gun belts, saddles, sandals, shoes, belts, bags and pouches, in common use by both Baluch and Brahvi groups. Leather is dyed dark-red or brown and embroidered in a delicate chain stitch (see figs. 120, 121).

Woven Textiles Pottinger, describing an encounter with a Bizenjo chief at the court of the Jam of Las Bela in 1816, wrote: "They were all dressed in the same manner as their chiefs, with a loose white cotton shirt which came below the knees, a pair of trowsers of blue or striped cotton and a small round cap which sat close to the head; the only distinction I perceived was in their horses and accoutrements; and when Ruhmut Khan visited the Jam he tied a *Loongee* round his waist, an article of dress to which none of his attendants aspired."[7] He describes the Jam as wearing an "*Ulkhaliq* of red Keemkhwab with a white turband of considerable dimensions".[8] Silk-weaving continues today in parts of Makran, where formerly a silk textile with a woven tartan pattern called the *manobas* was traditionally used as a male turban, a waistband or tied across the chest. A dark green silk and cotton cloth with a red border called *gushan* is still made into scarves and shawls for women, employing imported silk yarn from Iran. Magnificent turban cloths (*lungis*) using coloured silk with gold-wrapped thread were popular with tribal chieftains (notably the Khans of Kalat) for ceremonial wear. Many of these have now been replaced by commercially made silk in black and varying shades of grey.

Coarse cotton cloth (*bist dasti*) and woven cotton bedding (*khes*) is produced in Kach and Kalat. Finely woven cotton tied on the head in a variety of ways (*dastar*) helps to distinguish between tribes. The Bugti turban, for example, is made of a fine white muslin, 8–10 m long, and carefully wrapped around an embroidered *topi* (see figs. 118, 119). In Sibi, prayer mats, ropes, sacks, baskets, camel saddles, sandals (*sawas*) and matting for summer tents are all woven from the dwarf palm, *peesh* (*Nannerhops ritchiena*).

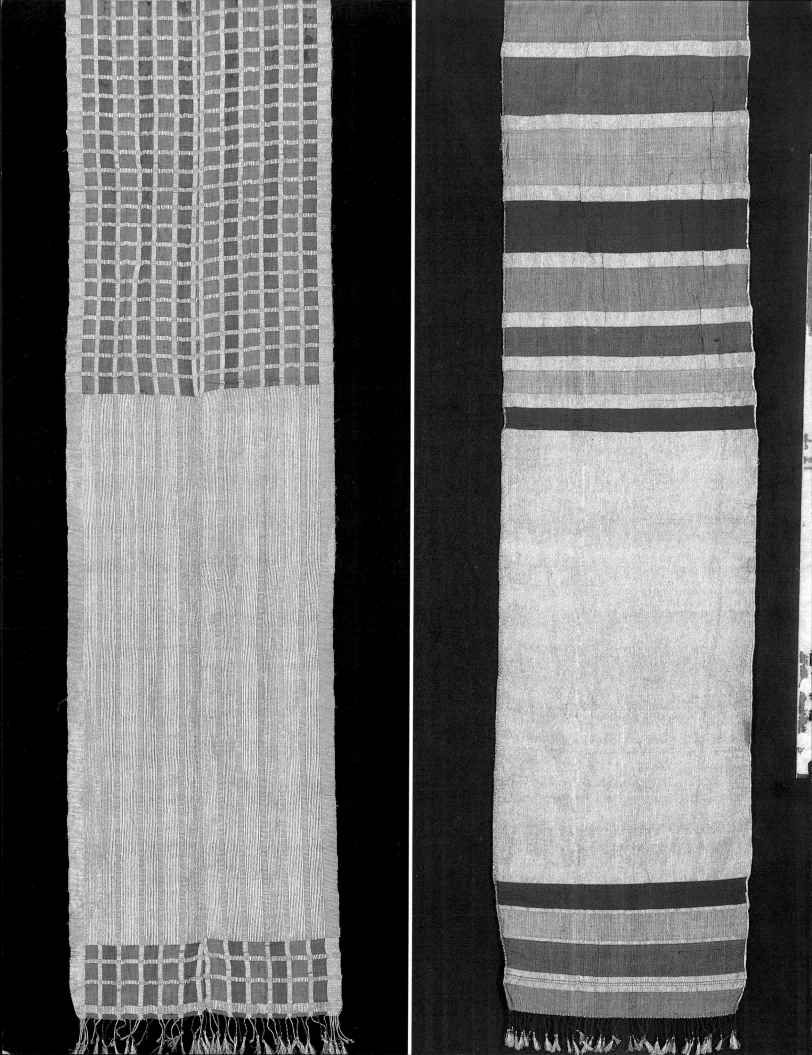

FAR LEFT 122 Man's turban-cloth or shoulder-wrap (*lungi*), probably from Makran, early 20th century (Victoria and Albert Museum T.231-1957). Silk woven with gold thread. L. 655 cm, W. 43 cm. Ornately woven cloths such as this were worn by tribal chiefs on ceremonial occasions as turbans or sashes over gathered tunics, *kurti*.

LEFT 123 Man's turban-cloth or shoulder-wrap (*lungi*), probably from Makran, early 20th century (Victoria and Albert Museum T.232-1957). Silk woven with gold thread. L. 210 cm, W. 39 cm. The field of this intricately woven *lungi* is made up of magenta and green silk warp threads with gold-wrapped threads in the weft. The ends have densely woven gold panels and the pattern of checks seen in the field is repeated in the borders.

ABOVE 124 Woven silk and cotton fabric (*khes*), from Turbat, west Baluchistan, *ca.* 1872 (Victoria and Albert Museum 9184 IS). L. 146 cm, W. 67 cm. K*hes* like this large piece made up of smaller fragments were commonly used as spreads in Baluchistan. An original paper label on this piece reads in English "Presented by the Governor of Turbat 11th April 1872". It was given to the India Museum in 1872 by a General Goldsmid, and the records state that it was presented to him "during the mission to Seistan".

RIGHT 125 Man's turban-cloth or shoulder-wrap (*lungi*), probably from Kalat, late 19th century (collection F. Samee). Silk woven with gold-wrapped thread, silk tassels and braid. L. 530 cm, W. 38 cm.

Woollen Textiles In the districts of Kalat, Quetta and Pishin, sheep's wool is used for felts (*namda* or *thappur*), rugs (*daris*), carpets (*galeecho*), saddle bags (*khurzeen*) and caps.[9] Felts are made primarily for domestic use as floorspreads, horse and camel blankets, bags, hats, winter coats, capes and waistcoats. The wool is beaten with sticks and carded until it is clean. It is then evenly spread on woven mats or dampened sheets of cloth and sprinkled with a soapy water mix. Layer upon layer of wool is built up until the desired thickness is obtained. Brightly dyed tufts of wool are then inserted symmetrically into the top layer to form patterns. The wool and mat are rolled up tightly, rotated backwards and forwards using pressure, and the roll is securely tied. This manipulation allows the dampened fibres of wool to bind together or interlace in a solid layer which is then opened out to dry and harden.

Goat's hair is used to weave blankets that are stretched over wooden poles to make large tents (*gidaan*), and for animal girths, storage bags, ropes and a variety of animal trappings. Beautiful woollen rugs and bags using floating and supplementary weft techniques are made by nearly all the nomadic groups. The simplest version is the plain, narrow *khat konth*, used as bedding or as a floor rug and the most elaborately patterned is a long runner or curtain used to cover bedding and cushions stacked in the nomads' tents (*shiffi*). Particularly fine examples of

ABOVE 126 Man's loose tunic (*kurta*), mid 19th century (Victoria and Albert Museum 6057 IS). Silk with gold braid around the neck opening. L. 82.5 cm, W. 61 cm.

BELOW 127 Man's quilted silk robe, probably from Kalat, mid 19th century (Victoria and Albert Museum 05521a IS). Woven silk, padded with cotton, with silk lining. L. 135 cm, W. across sleeves 94 cm. This robe shows a distinct Central Asian influence and would have been worn over a gathered cotton tunic (*kurti*) fastened above the waist.

RIGHT ABOVE 128 Man's robe (*kurti*), Khetran group, Barkhan village, Sulaiman range, late 19th century (collection Nawab Akbar Khan Bugti). Cotton with cotton embroidery and cotton tassels. L. 125 cm, W. across sleeves 190 cm. This traditional *kurti* was worn with gathered white cotton trousers (*shalwar*) and a cotton turban (*pag*).

RIGHT BELOW 129 Nawab Ghulam Murtaza Khan Bugti (centre) with his sons in traditional Bugti costume, Quetta, 1915

shiffi are made in Kharan and Sarawan (see figs. 136, 137). As most of the weaving is done on horizontal ground-looms that are transported on the backs of animals the weaves are generally less than a metre in width and two separate widths are often sewn together.

Girls begin to weave at an early age as women are primarily responsible for all forms of domestic weaving. They appear to weave from memory, and work singly or in pairs on looms with tripod frames that are set up and taken down as time permits. The design repertoire is essentially geometric, with both undyed and dyed wool used in restrained but striking colour combinations. White- or ivory-coloured goat's wool is used to lustrous effect in borders, or to highlight individual motifs as a contrast with the traditional

dark red, blue and brown of the field designs. Baluch rugs are traditionally known for their sparing colour palettes and fine repeating field designs, a particularly well known form of which includes patterned weft-faced bands alternating with bands of knotted pile. The ends of rugs are often left woven flat, a distinguishing feature. Prayer rugs usually have arch forms (*mihrabs*) or a small square at one end leading off from a larger central square. Ornamental borders are always a feature and vary in number and width. Today, a number of village and urban workshops (see fig. 134) produce flat-weaves and pile rugs in vivid colour combinations and patterns specifically for sale in bazaar towns.

Saddle bags (*khurzeen*) with complex geometric patterns are woven by both men and women with camel, goat and sheep's wool (see fig. 130). Bags used to store grain (*gwalug*), flour (*toorag*) and salt (*wadaan*) are often decorated with shells from the Makran coast, woollen tassels, bindings and braids. Clothes and vessels are kept and carried by the nomads in cleverly constructed braided wool bags (*sikka* or *takki*), also known as *balisht* when they are woven in pairs for loading on the backs of animals. Woollen shawls for women and woollen capes and coats for men (*zor* or *shul*) vary considerably in texture and are often brightly embellished with silk embroidery. Fabric for waistcoats (*sadri*) made from the wool of fat-tailed sheep (*ispet-nas*) is woven in Turbat and Makran where it is commonly referred to as Makrani *patti*.

130 Saddle bag (*khurzeen*), probably Rakhshani group, Chagai, mid 20th century (collection N. Askari). White wool ground with patterned bands in weft-faced, slit tapestry, supplementary weft and wrapped weft (*soumak*) techniques. Loops and fastenings of plaited black goat's hair. L. 147 cm, W. 66 cm.

131 Nomad woman wearing an elaborately embroidered dress (*pashk*) weaving a colourful floor rug (*konth*) on a ground-loom outside her tent, Mastung Road, near Quetta, 1996

132 Brahvi woman weaving a saddle-bag (*khurzeen*) outside Quetta, 1996

133 Mengal boys holding up a brightly decorated felt, Dringal group, near Quetta, 1996

134 Boy weaving a floor rug in a village workshop, Bibi Nani, Bolan Pass, 1996

136 A Chagai woman in her tent, Mastung Road, near Quetta, 1996. Behind her is a pile of bedding covered with a *shiffi* and other rugs including one edged with shells and bead amulets.

135 Floor-cover (*konth*), Bangulzai group, Isplinji, Sarawan, early 20th century (British Museum (Dept. of Ethnography) 1970 AS 21.6). Wool with repeating geometric patterns in bands, including one with stylized camels. L. 240 cm, W. 108 cm.

137 Detail of a rug used as bedding cover (*shiffi*), Zaggar Mengal group, Nushki Chagai, early 20th century (British Museum (Dept. of Ethnography) 1970 AS 21.8). Wool, woven with supplementary weft patterns. L. 361 cm, W. 124 cm.

138 Nomadic Baluch singers wearing loose tunics (*kurtas*), gathered trousers (*shalwar*) and embroidered waistcoats (*sadri*), reciting a folk tale, Lok Virsa Festival, Islamabad, 1997

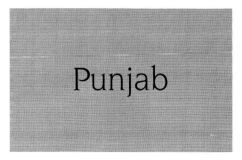

Punjab

Punjab is named after thc five rivers that flow through it: the Jhelum, Chenab, Ravi and Sutlej and its tributary, the Beas. It is the richest province of Pakistan and the most densely populated, with some 60 million inhabitants. Its fertile plains have ensured continuous prosperity, and the area has been inhabited since at least the Harappan period (*ca.* 2000 BC), and probably longer. Lahore, the main city of Punjab, is believed to have been founded in about 1000 BC, and in more recent times has been a centre of Muslim culture for the whole of the subcontinent. It has been a capital of the Mughals and Sikhs, and was a major centre of British administration in pre-Partition India. Almost as significant in cultural terms is the city of Multan, which was attacked by Alexander the Great in *ca.* 326 BC. A centre of Islam since the eighth century, Multan has historic links with Iran and Afghanistan, and is especially known for the beautifully decorated tombs of Muslim saints and holy men (see fig. 139). Other cities, such as Jhang and Bahawalpur, have also contributed to the cultural history of Punjab, in which textiles play an important part.

Woven cotton and silk, embroidery and block-printing have all been major elements in the textile production of the Punjab. All of these have undergone huge changes over the last hundred years and some have died out completely in some areas. Fortunately, nineteenth- and early twentieth-century accounts exist of the many textile processes of the day, examples of most of which were collected for what was then the South Kensington Museum, now the Victoria and Albert Museum.

Woven Cotton Textiles Cotton is a major crop of the Punjab, and woven cottons have traditionally formed a very significant proportion of its textile output. These were generally of a somewhat coarse type for local use (although some cotton cloths were

139 Tomb of Bibi Jawindi, 1493, Uchh Sharif

exported to Kabul)[1] as garment pieces, like the plain *khadar* cloth, and bedding, like *khes*. *Khes* (see also Sindh chapter) was once produced in huge quantities by hand, but is now mostly woven on power-looms. Although it is perhaps more frequently associated with Sindh, where finer varieties are woven at centres such as Nasarpur, Punjab also has a long tradition of *khes*-weaving, and many references to it are made by nineteenth-century writers.

The term *khes* is today often used both in the West and in Pakistan as the specific name for the thick, checked cotton fabric of Sindh and Punjab, although this has not always been the case. Its local usage seems to be a generic one for a thick cotton fabric with a twill weave used as bedding, and in some areas also for a particular type of plain white cotton cloth with a simple blue stripe along the borders. The precise meaning is not clarified by commentators such as J. Lockwood Kipling, writing in the *Journal of Indian Art* in the late nineteenth century, or George Watt, in his catalogue of the exhibition of Indian art and manufactures held in Delhi in 1903, who both use the term to refer to several different textiles. Kipling even refers to "dun-coloured *khes*", which he distinguishes from *khadar*, "the coarse white cloth worn by agriculturalists"[2] (which is actually more likely to be found in shades of brown than white). In another section of the same survey, however, he defines the *khes* made in Jhang as "a stout, well-woven chequered fabric usually in indigo blue and white thread", much as we would recognize the term today. He also adds that "sometimes madder red is used instead of blue, but there are never more than two colours. From its exceptional substance this cloth makes a good cold weather wrap, and it is also used as a bed-quilt."[3] Surprisingly, Kipling does not mention any cotton *khes* being made in Multan, which is traditionally regarded as its main source in the Punjab, and where it is still made today, but he refers to a silk variety made there as "a sort of checked, damasked fabric".[4] Silk *khes* is still made in several parts of Sindh and Punjab. All the examples of cotton *khes* selected by J. Forbes Watson for his sample books, completed in 1867, are from Sindhi rather than Punjabi weaving centres.[5]

When *khes* is used today in the Punjab in the general sense of thick cotton bedding fabric, the more complex fabric woven in double-cloth technique with a distinctive checked design is specifically called *chandni khes* or *majnu khes*.[6] This type of geometrically patterned double-cloth came into its own with the adoption of the jacquard-loom, apparently from Varanasi in India early this century,[7] which enabled complex designs to be woven more easily and on a more compact loom than the traditional pit-loom. A closely related type of checked cotton cloth with a woven diamond pattern is called *gumti khes* (see figs. 61, 62, 64 in Sindh chapter).[8]

The commonly found striped cotton cloth called *soosi* is traditionally used for women's trousers (*shalwar*). It is made in parts of Sindh and the Punjab, and today is frequently found in a mixture of synthetic and cotton yarns.

Cotton was also used for the important *dari*-weaving industry of the Punjab. These flat-woven cotton rugs were frequently made in villages by women of each household, for use as bedding and floor-coverings. Larger centres such as Lahore, Multan and Bahawalpur were known for their large, boldly patterned *daris*, often in blue-and-white geometric designs, which were commissioned for local mosques and interiors. Many of the finest *daris* were made not by professional craftsmen but by prisoners in jails: in the Punjab, the jails at Multan (see fig. 140) and Sahiwal (formerly Montgomery) were especially noted for their *daris*, but prisons in Sindh and many other parts of the subcontinent were also producing fine examples.[9] Although the complete history of *dari*-weaving in the Punjab is unclear, a tentative link with the golden age of Mughal carpet-weaving is provided by the splendid, if fragmentary, flat-woven carpet now in the Calico Museum in Ahmedabad, India (although it is not technically a *dari* as the wefts are of wool), which is thought to have been woven in Lahore in the seventeenth century.[10]

Woven Silk Textiles

Although the Punjab is well known for several types of silk textile, silk has not traditionally been cultivated there on a sufficiently large scale to support its weaving industry.[11] The silk fabrics woven there were formerly made of silk yarn imported from Bukhara and Khorasan, and also from Bengal in India, but these sources did not survive the competition of Chinese and, later, Japanese silks, which are softer and easier to dye.

The plain and striped silks woven at Lahore in brilliant combinations of pink and yellow or green and red (see fig. 141) were made of Bukhara silk, often with a shot effect (*dhup-chaon* or 'light and shade') produced by using warps and wefts of different colours. Bukhara silk has a distinctive 'hard' feel unlike the softer Far Eastern yarn, and produces a much stiffer finished cloth. These fabrics were produced as yardage to be made up into garments, especially trousers, and for the linings of robes.

More elaborate are the splendid *lungis* woven in the Punjab and North-West Frontier Province (NWFP). *Lungi* is a term which can be applied to both waistcloths and turbans depending on the locality, but in Punjab refers only to waistcloths, while a turban is called *pag* (see figs. 149, 150). Many of these *lungis* are of extremely high quality, both in materials and in weaving (see figs. 142, 143, 148), and they were woven in all the major towns of the Punjab, as well as NWFP and Sindh. Silk waistcloths called *lacha* are still woven in towns such as Bhera and Jhang: they typically have a bright-pink field with a wide bright-blue or green border, and are frequently embellished with woven gold patterns (see fig. 144).[12] Older silk *lungis*, such as those in the Victoria and Albert Museum's collection from Lahore and Multan, often have a plain field with only the horizontal gold band for decoration; others have checked fields (see fig. 143), while a more elaborate type is woven in a complex diamond pattern, sometimes in reversible colours (see fig. 146).

Simpler but equally elegant *lacha*, with a cotton field, often checked, and silk borders are still woven in several places. *Salara*, a large cloth used as a woman's head-covering, may be striped, checked or with a plain field. The related *salari* is a large silk shawl traditionally associated with towns such as Kalabagh, Khushab, Shahpur and Sargodha in the north of the Punjab (see fig. 145). These large cloths of multicoloured silk were widely worn in the Punjab, although they are now rare. The use of brilliantly coloured plain, checked or striped silk was formerly typical of women's dress in the Punjab, and combinations such as vivid pink, purple, green and yellow

140 Flat-woven rug (*dari* or *dhurrie*), cotton, made in Multan Jail in about 1880 (Victoria and Albert Museum 2457-1883 IS). L. 220 cm, W. 135 cm. Although many such rugs were made in villages for domestic use, some of the finest quality *daris* were made by the inmates of jails.

ABOVE 141 Four lengths of silk, woven in Lahore in about 1850 from silk imported from Bukhara (Victoria and Albert Museum). LEFT TO RIGHT: (7191 IS) W. 54.5 cm; (0781 IS) W. 55.5 cm, L. 696 cm; (7163 IS) W. 54.8 cm, L. 278 cm; (0795 IS) W. 54.6, L. 856 cm. Brilliantly coloured silks, both plain and striped, were used for making garments, especially trousers (*shalwar*), and as lining and edging material.

FAR LEFT 142 Waist-cloth (*lungi* or *lacha*) of silk and gold-wrapped thread, woven in the Punjab in about 1850 (Victoria and Albert Museum 7109 IS). W. 76.5 cm. The brilliant colour scheme of pink, green and gold is typical of the silk textiles of the Punjab.

LEFT 143 Waist-cloth (*lungi* or *lacha*) of silk and cotton with gold-wrapped thread end border, from Rawalpindi, *ca.* 1855 (Victoria and Albert Museum 6004 IS). L. 472 cm, W. 77 cm. The field has a pattern of tiny woven checks.

in one outfit were favoured (see fig. 147).

The silk-weaving industry of Multan, which was once one of the largest in the Punjab, has now diminished to the point where the only silk textile still woven there by hand is the turban of olive-green or black silk favoured by Afghan men. These distinctive five-metre-long turbans known as *lungi* or *mashaddi*, originally from Mashhad in Iran, are woven from Chinese silk (although the black ones are frequently synthetic) and are bought mainly by Afghans living in Pakistan, who can be seen on the streets of Peshawar and Quetta with the long ends hanging down over their shoulders.

A small but significant element of the silk industry, especially in Multan and Lahore, was the production of the elaborately patterned drawstrings (*ezarband*) for trousers (see figs. 152, 153, 154). These were traditionally of fine silk, woven in the interlacing technique known as sprang, which produces a mesh-like textile, often with a diamond pattern formed of spaces in the weaving. The *ezarband* is constructed by stretching the silk yarns over a wooden cross-piece, usually wedged across the frame of a *charpai* (bed), and manipulating the yarns into a mesh while keeping them separate by means of reed sticks.[13] It would usually be further

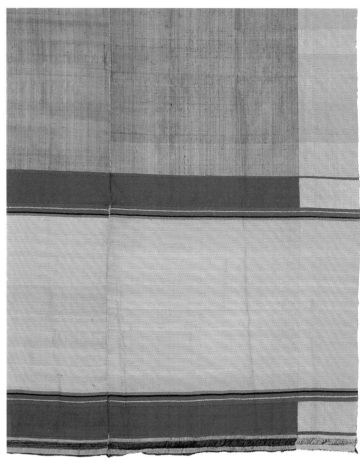

TOP LEFT 144 Waist-cloth (*lacha*) of silk and gold-wrapped thread, made in Kartalpur, Punjab, *ca.* mid 20th century (collection Fauzia Khawar Ali Shah)

TOP RIGHT 145 Woman's shawl (*salari*) of shot blue and green silk, woven in Kalabagh, Punjab, *ca.* 1930–40 (collection F. Samee). L. 272 cm, W. 142 cm. Large shawls such as this would be wrapped around the head and entire body, and worn with equally brilliantly coloured *kurta* and *shalwar*.

LEFT 146 Piece of silk fabric woven so that the surface and the reverse are of two different colours, Punjab, mid 19th century (Victoria and Albert Museum 7265a IS).

RIGHT 147 Woman's outfit of shirt (*kurta*), wrapper (*lacha*) and shawl (*dupatta*) of woven silk, Punjab, *ca.* 1930–40 (collection F. Samee)

FACING PAGE 148 Part of a waist-cloth (*lungi*), probably from Bahawalpur, mid 19th century (Victoria and Albert Museum 7239a IS). Woven silk with gold-wrapped thread end border.

149 Turban-cloth (*pag*), probably from the Punjab, mid 19th century (Victoria and Albert Museum 5931 IS). Woven silk with gold-wrapped silk ends. W. 24.2 cm. This remarkable turban has been woven with double warps and wefts of red and green silk, which are woven together to give a shot effect until the final section of the fabric, when the two sets of warps and wefts are woven separately to produce double ends of single colours.

embellished with elaborate knots, tassels and fringes, in either silk or gold thread and frequently tablet-woven,[14] which would hang down from the waist.

Woven Woollen Textiles The weaving of woollen cloth is not as important in the Punjab as in other areas, especially the cold regions of the north, but the province's proximity to Kashmir has given woollen textiles a greater prominence than they might otherwise have received. With the great famine in Kashmir in 1833, shawl-weavers were forced down to the plains, where their skills gave impetus to the shawl-weaving industry in several centres, particularly Lahore. The Punjabi shawls never attained the quality of their Kashmiri equivalents, partly because of the lack of fine *pashmina* goat's hair to weave, but plainer woollen shawls were produced that were of reason-

150 Turban-cloth (*pag*), probably made in the Punjab, mid 19th century (Victoria and Albert Museum 5929 IS). Red silk with woven gold-wrapped thread end borders. L. 964 cm.

RIGHT 151 Length of silk yardage made in Bahawalpur, *ca.* 1855 (Victoria and Albert Museum 0794 IS). L. 496 cm, W. 73 cm. Luxurious silk fabric like this would be used for making trousers (*shalwar*).

FAR RIGHT 152 Decorative cord (*ezarband*) for a pair of trousers (*shalwar*), made in Lahore, *ca.* 1850 (Victoria and Albert Museum 0201 IS). Silk in the sprang technique, with gold tassels. L. 272 cm. The tassels are detachable so that the *ezarband* may be threaded through the waistband.

able quality. One of the more attractive woollen products of Lahore was the plain, undyed shawl with narrow red or green silk borders (see fig. 157), which sadly appears to have died out. The brightly coloured edging survives, however, in the bright green borders of the traditional plain shawls of several centres of the North-West Frontier, notably Swat and Peshawar. The felted woollen cloth called *malida*, used for garments and furnishing, was also produced in Lahore and was exported all over India.[15]

Woollen pile carpets have played a prominent part in the textile history of the Punjab. Lahore was well known as one of the major centres of carpet-weaving during the Mughal period (see Introduction), but it may be that the constant trade between Lahore and Multan and the carpet-weaving centres of Iran and Afghanistan established a tradition of carpet-weaving even before the emperor Akbar set up his carpet workshops in Lahore in the late sixteenth century. With such a pedigree it is surprising that the carpet industry seems to have declined almost to extinction by the late nineteenth century, with the exception of some production in the prisons.[16] It was only after Partition in 1947 that pile-carpet-weaving, which today is a major element of Pakistan's economy, began to be revived, largely as a result of the influx of Muslim weavers from Indian centres such as Mirzapur and Amritsar as well as Kashmir. Assisted by government schemes for training and marketing, there are now thousands of workshops all over Pakistan, with the majority in Punjab.[17] Most of the carpets are woven to designs based on Turkmen, Baluch or classical Iranian patterns.

Embroidery Perhaps the best known of all textiles from the Punjab is *phulkari* embroidery. Unlike the woven textiles, *phulkari* is essentially a domestic textile, made by a non-professional embroiderer in her home, for herself or for her own family. While some rich patrons might employ embroiderers in their households to make fine *phulkari*, these were not traditionally items to be bought and sold in the bazaar, but given as gifts at auspicious events, especially weddings.[18]

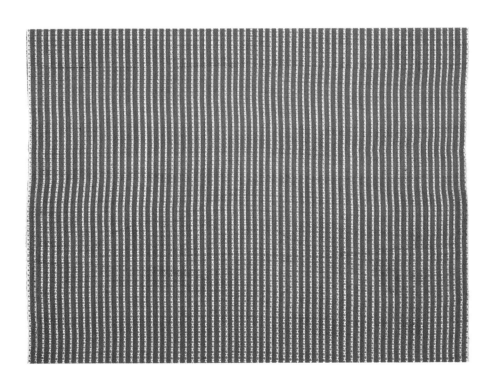

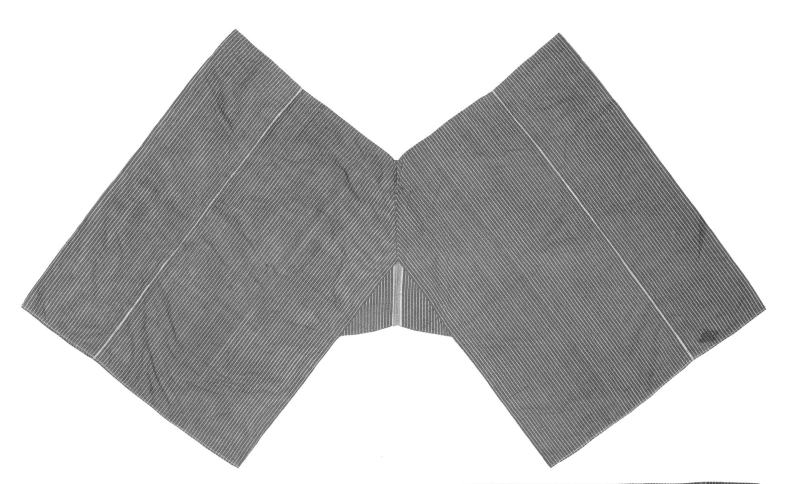

TOP LEFT 153 Pair of trousers (*shalwar*) of Lahore silk, mid 19th century (Victoria and Albert Museum 05595 IS)

BELOW LEFT 154 Pair of trousers of Lahore silk, mid 19th century (Victoria and Albert Museum 05643:4 IS)

ABOVE 155 Women's trousers of Lahore silk, acquired in Peshawar, mid 19th century (Victoria and Albert Museum 05548 IS). Probably worn in tribal areas of NWFP.

RIGHT 156 Women's trousers (*suthan*), probably from Sindh, mid 19th century (Victoria and Albert Museum 6047 IS). Silk with embroidered cuffs.

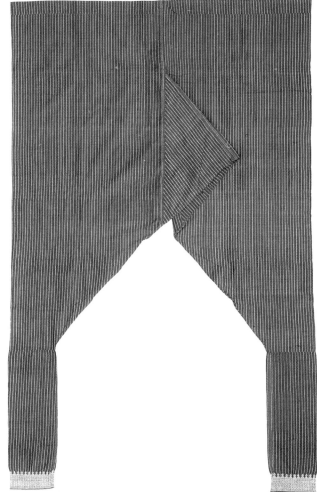

Phulkari were traditionally made all over the Punjab, on both the Indian and the Pakistani side of the post-Partition border, and also further north in Hazara district, where some of the finest types were made (see NWFP chapter). Made and used by both Muslim and Hindu communities,[19] *phulkari* of either society differ to some degree: those made by Hindu embroiderers in the eastern Punjab (now in India), for example, tend to incorporate figurative designs of people, animals and household implements, while the Muslim communities of the western Punjab (now mostly in Pakistan) confine themselves to non-figurative geometric patterns (see fig. 158). Originally an art of rural communities, *phulkari* (which means 'flower work') were embroidered in floss silk thread

157 Piece of a woollen shawl with a silk edge, woven in Lahore, *ca.* 1850, page from J. Forbes Watson's *Textile Manufactures of India*, London 1867 (XVIII, no. 689).

Detail of fig. 158 (opposite) showing the reverse of the fabric. *Phulkari* embroidery is worked from the back of the piece, and only the smallest possible amount of silk shows on the reverse.

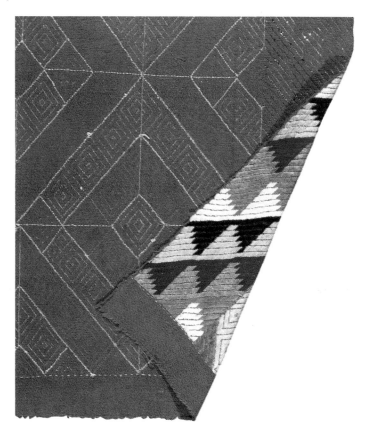

(*pat*) on coarse local cotton fabric (*khaddar*). This ground fabric was usually dyed with madder to a deep reddish-brown[20] or sometimes an indigo blue (see fig. 159), and the embroidery was almost always in yellow or white.[21] At its most basic level for everyday use, the embroidery would consist of simple flower shapes dotted over the fabric of the full skirts (*ghaghra*) or the large all-enveloping head-covers (*chadar*) traditionally worn by rural Punjabi women. More elaborate types called *bagh* ('garden') also evolved for use as ceremonial gifts. These used far more silk, as the entire surface of the cotton ground would frequently be completely covered with embroidered geometric patterns (as in fig. 158). While the colours of the embroidery silk would usually still be confined to yellow and white even for these *bagh*, bright flashes of pink, purple and green were sometimes added, especially along the border framing the face when in use.

The most remarkable feature of the *phulkari* is that it is worked entirely from the reverse of the fabric, so that the embroiderer does not (or need not) see the front while she is creating the pattern. The rigid geometry of the *bagh* pattern is produced by counting the threads on the reverse of the ground fabric, which is fortunately of a fairly coarse yarn and loose weave, before taking up a single thread with the needle, leaving a long 'float' of silk on the front (see detail of reverse of fig. 158).

Even when Flora Annie Steel was writing in 1888, the art of *phulkari* was evidently under severe threat, mainly from imported (British) cotton cloth and embroidery thread. It survived, however, well into the twentieth century, although not perhaps with the variety or quality that Mrs Steel had known. With the massive changes in society brought about by Partition and by increased industrialization, *phulkari* was one of many domestic arts that had become irrelevant to modern society, even in rural communities. The dowry system had also undergone radical changes and household goods and factory-made

FACING PAGE 158 Woman's shawl (*phulkari chadar*), cotton embroidered with floss silk (Victoria and Albert Museum IS 3-1961). L. 234 cm, W. 128 cm. This type of dense, geometric *phulkari* embroidery, called *bagh* or garden, is typical of the western Punjab (now in Pakistan).

159 Skirt, indigo-dyed cotton embroidered in floss silk and embellished with mirrors (Victoria and Albert Museum 05668 IS). L. 96 cm, W. at waist 48.5 cm. This skirt uses a less refined type of *phulkari* embroidery than the *chadar* (fig. 158). It was recorded as coming from Bannu in NWFP in the mid 19th century, although the style of embroidery is much closer to that of the Punjab than the fine Hazara *phulkaris* of NWFP.

clothing were now seen as far more desirable than hand-embroidered *phulkari*, which was seen as coarse and unfashionable.

Embroidery done by professionals, usually men, in cities such as Lahore and Multan, however, has had a relatively stable history. In Lahore a variety of the Kashmiri style of chain-stitch embroidery was used both in silk and gold thread to embellish robes (*choga*) and caps. This was usually applied to woollen garments such as those in figs. 160 and 161, exactly as it would have been in Kashmir itself. Figurative embroidery such as this was done for both Sikh and Muslim patrons in the nineteenth century (Lahore was capital of the Sikh-ruled Punjab until the British annexed it in 1849): the figures on some embroidered robes of this type can be identified as Sikh by their distinctive beards and turbans, while other examples show scenes from Persian legend. Non-figurative, scrolling patterns derived from Kashmir shawl designs also occur (fig. 161). Kashmir-style embroidery continues to be done on shawls in several parts of northern Punjab and Azad Kashmir. Lahore continues as an important centre for embroidery in silk and gold thread, using a repertoire of decorative elements such as beads and sequins.

Multan has today become known as a centre for fine professional embroidery of several types, usually worked on a frame by several embroiderers, generally young men or boys, working together (fig. 164). The pattern may be in coloured silk thread worked with an awl (*ari*) in chain stitch on fine muslin for *dupattas* and *kurtas*, or in gold thread on silk for weddings. A type of white-on-white embroidery derived from the *chikan* work of Lucknow is also much in demand for *kurtas* and *dupattas*. The areas around Dera Ghazi Khan are known for their drawn-thread work (*thar kashi*) and fine embroidery on muslin done from the reverse side of the cloth (*kacha tanka*).

Embroidery and appliqué work using ribbon woven of silk and gold-wrapped thread (*gota*; see figs. 162 and 163) was formerly associated with the erstwhile princely state of Bahawalpur, which adjoins Rajasthan on its eastern side. Although since its foundation in the eighteenth century the state was ruled by Muslim *nawabs*, Bahawalpur had much in common with the Hindu Rajput states, especially its nearest neighbour Bikaner, and the use of gold *gota* is very much a part of the Rajasthani court style.[22] *Gota* applied to tie-dyed cotton cloth was also a speciality of the Bahawalpur state, especially the Cholistan Desert region. This is an extension of the Thar Desert which straddles the Sindh–Rajasthan border, and tie-dyeing is to be found on both sides of the Pakistan border in this area (see figs. 167, 168).

Multan and Lahore, as well as the nearby town of Sharaqpur, are traditionally known for finely embroidered shoes (*jooti* or *khussa*; figs. 165, 166). While *jooti* is a generic term for shoes of all traditional types, the *khussa* is the traditional round-toed slipper. When the toe is curled up to a fine point the shoe is called *salimshahi*, after the Mughal emperor Jahangir (formerly Prince Salim) who supposedly made them fashionable. Both types are frequently lavishly embroidered with gold or silver thread (*tilla*). The embroidery of the upper is done over a cut-paper design which is pasted on to the leather as a guide. While in some workshops the embroidery is done by the craftsmen who cut and stitch the leather components of the shoe, others farm it out to women in nearby villages who can complete the embroidery for one pair of shoes in a day. Elegant shoes like the *salimshahi* are made with cow-hide, but sturdier work shoes, like the robust, boat-like *jootis* of Cholistan, are more likely to be made of harder buffalo leather.

Fine embroidery on leather known as *kundi* work was traditionally produced, especially for use on gun-belts and their accoutrements, in a broad 'frontier' area spanning parts of the Punjab, NWFP and Baluchistan. Dera Ghazi Khan, Dera Ismail Khan and Quetta were all known for this type of fine silk embroidery (see fig. 120). Whatever the place of origin, embroidery of this type is almost always in patterns of small circles done in buttonhole and chain stitch, densely packed together on the leather ground.

TOP LEFT 160 Man's robe (*choga*), Lahore, mid 19th century (Victoria and Albert Museum 0200 IS). Red woollen fabric embroidered with gold- and silver-wrapped thread and lined with silk. H. 134 cm, W. at shoulders 39 cm. This robe is decorated with typical northern-Indian and Kashmiri motifs, such as the single flower in staggered rows and the *buti* (mango, cone or Paisley pattern) in the borders and corners.

LEFT 161 Man's robe (*choga*), made in Lahore, *ca.* 1850 (Victoria and Albert Museum 05597 IS). Wool embroidered in chain stitch with floss silk. L. 129 cm, W. at shoulders 41 cm. This type of elaborate embroidery originally evolved as an alternative to woven patterns for Kashmir shawls, but also came to be used on robes and sashes.

ABOVE Back of fig. 160

RIGHT Detail of back of fig. 161

162 Young man's robe (*angarkha*), Lahore, mid 19th century (Victoria and Albert Museum 05643a IS). Silk, with applied gold ribbon (*gota*) and silk lining at the hem and front opening. H. 111 cm, W. at shoulders 30 cm.

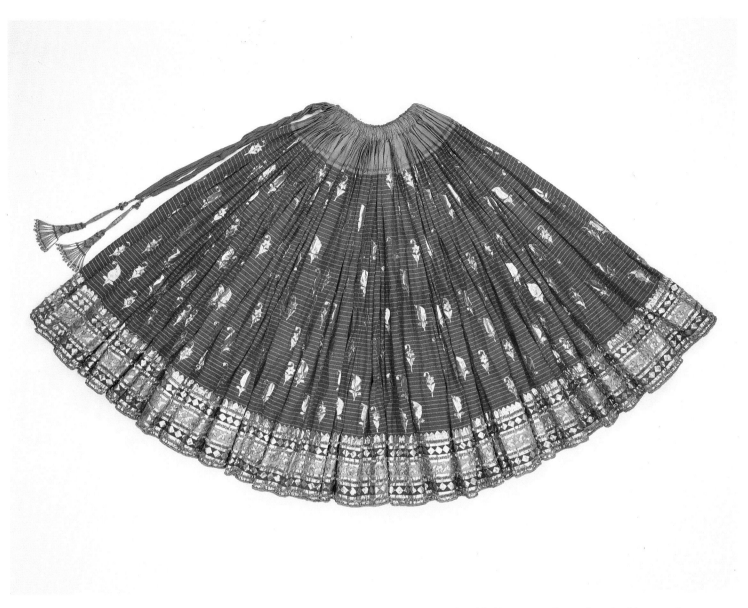

163 Skirt (Victoria and Albert Museum, 05845 IS). Lahore silk with appliqué *gota* work: gold ribbon woven from silk and gold-wrapped thread. L. 100 cm. *Gota* is used extensively as a decorative trim to garments, and is especially associated with the parts of Punjab bordering Rajasthan, especially Bahawalpur.

ABOVE 165 Pair of men's shoes (*jooti*), made in Sharaqpur, *ca*. 1996 (collection N. Askari). Leather embroidered with gold thread. Heavily embroidered shoes like these are still widely worn in Pakistan, especially on formal occasions. Plainer shoes, either with the turned-up toe or with a flat toe (*khussa*), are used for everyday wear.

LEFT 164 An embroidery workshop in Multan. A *dupatta*, probably for a wedding, is being ornately embroidered with gold-wrapped thread and sequins by a team of young professional embroiderers.

Block-Printing Block-printing on cotton continues to be carried out in several centres in the Punjab, with varying degrees of refinement. There appears to be no mention of printed fabrics from the region before the nineteenth century, although the finely painted chintzes of Multan were attracting attention as early as the late seventeenth century and continued to be highly prized throughout the eighteenth.[23] The main centres of cotton-printing were Lahore, Multan and Kot Kamalia (simply called Kamalia today) which lies between them. Other smaller centres include the small town of Kahror Pakka, between Multan and Bahawalpur.[24] None of the block-prints made today, or surviving from the nineteenth century, are as fine as the best *ajrak* prints from Sindh, for example. They are mostly for bedding and furnishing and are printed on coarser cotton than that used for garments, as in the case of *ajrak*. This coarser weave is not suitable for printing fine designs, so the patterns of the Punjabi block-prints have tended to be rather large in scale.

The main printed items were bed-covers, floor-

166 Pair of women's shoes (*jooti*) from Multan (collection Fauzia Khawar Ali Shah). Leather embroidered with gold thread.

ABOVE 168 Child's shirt (*kurta*), Jhelum, Punjab, mid 19th century (Victoria and Albert Museum 05449 IS). Tie-dyed cotton. L. 62 cm, W. across sleeves 110 cm.

LEFT 167 Part of a woman's shawl, probably from Cholistan, mid 19th century (Victoria and Albert Museum 5141 IS). Tie-dyed cotton. W. 80.5 cm, L. 244 cm. This is probably half of a rectangular shawl, made up of two pieces joined vertically.

spreads and wall-hangings. The most successful pieces, such as those made in Kamalia in about 1880, draw on architectural elements such as pillars and arches, with brightly coloured flowering plants and border patterns, typically in red, green and dark purple, filling the spaces. J.L. Kipling cites the printer Allah Yar as the best printer in the town,[25] and it is quite likely that the Victoria and Albert Museum's wall-hanging or screen (*dewalgir* or *qanat*; fig. 169) was made by him. The Kamalia prints were also augmented by the hand-colouring of some areas with a brush, but resist-dyeing is not used.[26]

The prints made in Lahore in the nineteenth and early twentieth century are characterized by a softer palette and somewhat finer ground cloth (fig. 170). The muted colours and less bold designs, drawing largely on Persian *kalamkari* designs rather than Punjabi architectural motifs, found favour especially with Europeans at that time, and many Lahore printed bedspreads can still be found in British homes. The printer Jhandu, whom Watt singles out for praise in his catalogue of 1903,[27] was apparently still working in 1933, when the curtain in fig. 170 was purchased from him by an Englishwoman in Lahore. Although

169 Block-printed cotton screen (*qanat*), made in Kamalia, Punjab, *ca.* 1880 (Victoria and Albert Museum IS 1811-1883). H. 99 cm, W. 556 cm. Long portable screens like this were used to form enclosures and could also be used as wall decoration. The design on this one uses architectural elements in late Mughal style.

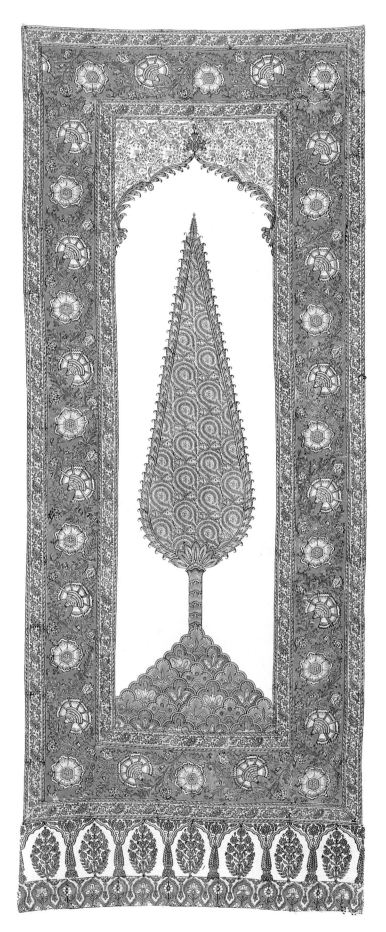

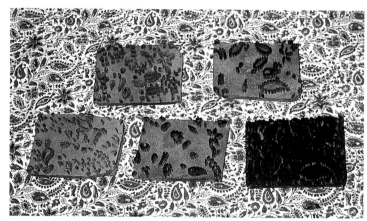

ABOVE 171 A block-printed cotton cloth from Kahror Pakka, Punjab, and the five blocks needed to make the complete pattern, 1996. The most densely carved block (bottom right) is used first, to provide the outline of the pattern, and the remaining four are used for one colour each.

LEFT 170 Block-printed cotton hanging, made in Lahore in about 1930 by Jhandu (Victoria and Albert Museum IS 129-1986). L. 224 cm, W. 87 cm. The floral design of the borders of this piece, and its colour range of ochre and pale blue, are typical of Lahore block-prints of the late 19th and early 20th century.

the design is stiff and the printing not of the finest quality, the colours and motifs are typical of the Lahore style of block-printing.

The Lahore tradition may be said to have been inherited today by the block-printers of Kahror Pakka, whose products also tend to be in a somewhat Persianate style. The fabrics are printed from finely carved blocks of *shisham*-wood in complex designs, with up to four different colours plus the black outline, each requiring a separate block (see fig. 171). The quality of the block-carving is high, and, with a little more attention paid to the printing itself, block-printing could be re-established as a major craft of the Punjab.

North-West Frontier Province

North-West Frontier Province is made up of a complex mosaic of peoples and landscapes which, though grouped together to form a single administrative region, retain much of their individual identities and cultures. The component parts of the Province include a narrow belt of tribal areas, the heartland of the Pathans, running along the frontier with Afghanistan; the almost parallel valleys of Chitral, Swat and the Indus running southwards from the Hindu Kush; the remote northern areas of Gilgit, Hunza and Baltistan dominated by the peaks of the Karakoram Mountains; and the Hazara district which links the plains of the Punjab to the highlands of Swat and Indus Kohistan. Outside these subdivisions remain anomalies such as the smaller valleys of Chitral which are the home of the isolated Kalash people, the only non-Muslim society for hundreds of miles.

Apart from an area of land that runs along the west bank of the Indus and borders on Baluchistan, the majority of the land in NWFP is high and mountainous, with steep valleys terraced into small fields for the cultivation of food crops (see fig. 172). In villages scattered all over this difficult terrain, wool-weaving and fine embroidery are carried out, especially in the Indus and Swat Valleys. Silk- and cotton-weaving were formerly considerable industries

172 The landscape of Indus Kohistan in the Kolai Valley, with terraced fields and scattered houses. The River Indus, locally called Abbasin, is visible in the distance.

173 Baltit Fort, Hunza. Baltit, dominated by Ultar Peak, is the old capital of Hunza. The Fort was the home of the Mirs of Hunza until the 1940s, when they moved to the new capital at Karimabad.

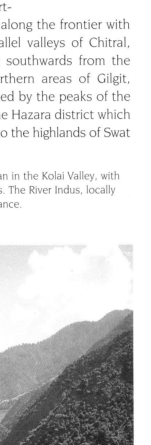

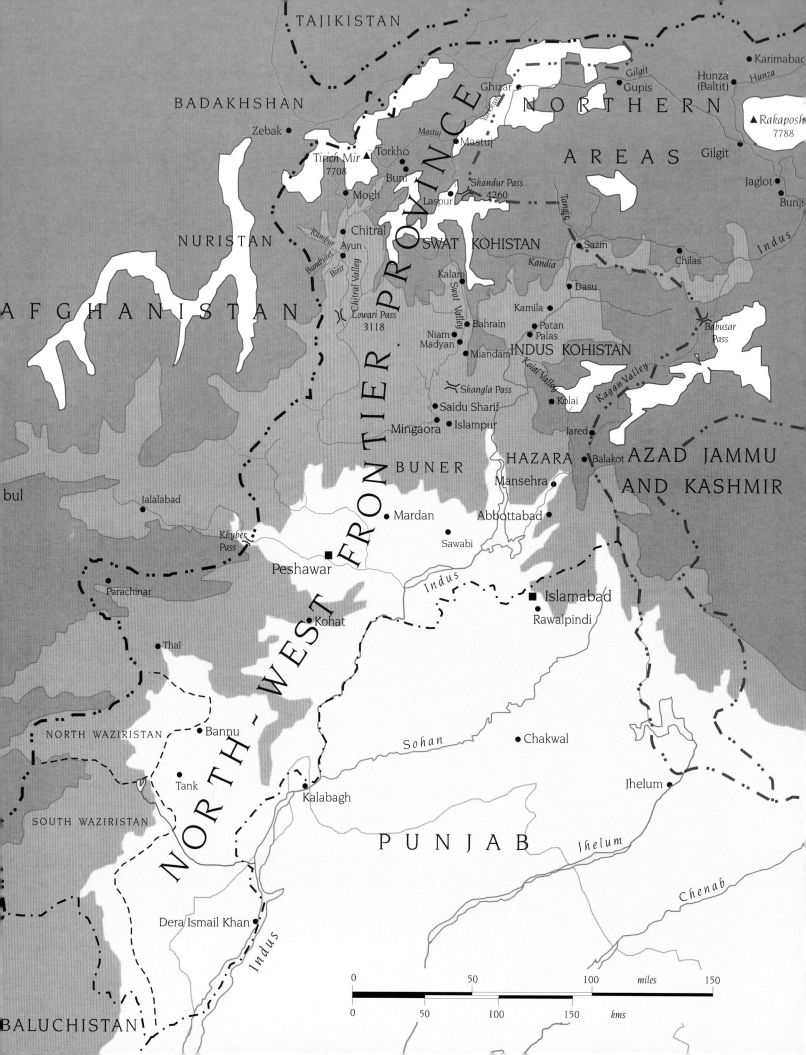

in towns in the lower regions, such as Kohat and Bannu, but have now largely been superseded by factory-made cloth from the larger cities.

Woven Textiles Woollen cloth plays a particularly important part in the life of hill people, and the weaving of wool for both shawls and the narrow lengths called *patti* is still carried out in many parts of the NWFP. Swat in particular is a long-established weaving centre, whose blankets (*kambal*) are mentioned in early Buddhist texts.[1] Today, shawls called *shari* are made at Islampur from local sheep's wool (often with an additional synthetic border), and other centres in the Swat Valley, together with Peshawar, Mansehra and Muzaffarabad, produce lightweight woollen blankets with coloured slit-tapestry borders which are used as shawls by men all over NWFP.

The most commonly used woollen cloth is the narrow, dense fabric called *patti*, which is woven in several centres of the northernmost parts of the Province. The remote village of Mogh, about 20 km north-west of Chitral in the Hindu Kush range, is well known as a wool-weaving centre. Here, local sheep's wool is used either in its undyed state (*khud rang*) to make an off-white *patti* cloth called *ishberu*, or dyed with walnuts in a range of brown shades to make rugs (also used as bedding) called *palesk* (see fig. 174) or a brown *patti* called *sho*, used for hats and waistcoats. Walnuts, which are a major feature of the local diet, are the only dye used in this area: both the shells and the nuts themselves yield the brown dye, and the bark of the walnut tree is also used if a stronger colour is required. A similar but plainer type of rug called *sharma* is woven in Hunza, in the far north-east of the Province: these are usually horizontally banded in undyed brown, grey and white, using the hair of the local goats and also of the yaks that are to be found in the valley in the winter.

The fine white woollen *patti* cloth woven in Hunza (see fig. 175) is called *zebaki*, after the town of Zebak in Badakhshan in Afghanistan, the home of the wife of a former *thum* or ruler. Tradition has it that she introduced weaving of this high quality to Hunza. *Zebaki* is woven in a dense weft-faced herringbone weave, which is also used for the slightly less tightly woven cloth employed for the traditional male robe worn in Hunza, called the *choga* or *shoka* (fig. 176). The finest of these robes were formerly woven from the hair of the wild ibex (*giri filam*), now extremely rare, rather than from sheep's wool (*belish filam*). The *choga* is of Central Asian origin, and has extra-long sleeves, often seen on garments from cold mountain regions, that can be pulled down to cover the hands for extra warmth. In Hunza, however, the coat is more often worn like a cape (see fig. 176), with the sleeves being used as a scarf to wrap around the neck in cold weather.[2] The Hunza *choga* is today frequently decorated with a brightly coloured embroidered flower on each side of the chest. Those found in Chitral are more likely to be of plain brown *patti*, but with machine-worked stiff lapels in the case of the 'Badakhshani' *choga* which is in popular use as a result of continuous contact with Afghanistan. It is also very close in shape to the padded silk *chapans* of northern Afghanistan and Uzbekistan.

As well as *chogas*, the local *patti* cloth is also used in the making of flat woollen caps (*pakol*) which are seen in subtly differing forms throughout northern Pakistan (see fig. 177). These caps are made by sewing a length of woollen cloth into a tube, adding a circular piece of cloth for the crown, placing it over a small bolster and rolling the fabric up to form a round brim. The Hunza cap is the least structured of the four main styles, with the crown of the hat left rounded and unstitched. In Chitral, the rim of the crown is given several rows of stitching to make the edge flatter and more pronounced; in Swat, a decorative 'pie-crust' effect is stitched into the rolled brim; and in the Kohistani style there is a somewhat deeper and flatter brim, which is stitched at intervals with vertical lines.

The hats are frequently adorned with ornaments ranging from simple flowers or grasses to the most elaborate feathered cap-badges (*gamburi*). The most sought-after decorations are those made of the feathers of the *monal* pheasant or *murgh-i zarin* ('golden bird') which lives in the neighbouring mountains. These iridescent green feathers are sometimes augmented by the longer plumes of the white crane, or the grey feathers of the snow-cock.

Woollen garments, especially coats, were formerly made and used in many parts of Kohistan ('land of

174 Flat-woven woollen rug (*palesk*), outside the home of its weaver in Mogh, Chitral, 1996. Local wool is dyed with walnuts in a variety of brown shades and used for weaving patterned rugs like this one. They are used as mattresses on *charpais* (beds) as well as floor rugs.

176 Woollen robe (*shoka*) worn as a cape in Baltit, Hunza Valley, 1996. The sleeves are rarely used, except to be wrapped around the neck like a scarf in cold weather.

175 Woollen *patti* cloth being woven in Karimabad, Hunza Valley, 1996. The thick, narrow cloth is woven on a simple loom, of which the members are decoratively carved. The cloth is used for hats, coats and waistcoats like those hanging up behind the weaver.

177 Woollen hats from the main valleys of the northern areas show small local variations in their design: these are from (left to right) Chitral, Swat, Kohistan and Hunza (Victoria and Albert Museum IS 5 to 8-1997).

178 Woollen embroidered coat, probably from Upper Chitral (Victoria and Albert Museum IS 37-1996). L. 104 cm, W. across sleeves 170 cm. Coats of this type are worn in the mountainous tract of land from Chitral across to Indus Kohistan and Gilgit.

179 Woollen embroidered coat, probably from Upper Chitral (Hiroko Iwatate Collection, Tokyo). L. 85 cm, W. across sleeves 135 cm. A more elaborate version of the coat in fig. 178.

mountains': the name given to the upper parts of the Swat and Indus Valleys) and the mountainous area linking Chitral to Gilgit (see figs. 178, 179). Made from densely woven and felted *patti* cloth, these coats are decorated with woollen embroidery, either in simple patterns of spots (for example, fig. 178) or in branching patterns, repeated on the woollen hats from the same areas (fig. 180). These branched or 'ram's horn' designs recall those on woollen garments and felts from Central Asia,[3] which is scarcely surprising in view of the continuous trade linking the northern areas of Pakistan with Central Asia: the valleys north of Chitral lead directly over passes into northern Afghanistan, China's most westerly province of Xinjiang and, perhaps most significantly, into the modern-day Republic of Tajikistan, where some textile traditions show marked parallels with those of northern Pakistan.

Woollen garments also form part of the traditional costume of the Kalash people, a dwindling non-Muslim group who are today confined to three valleys, Rumbur, Birir and Bumburet, which branch off the main Chitral Valley. They were formerly part of a larger community called the Kafirs ('non-believers')

180 Woollen embroidered hood from Upper Chitral (Victoria and Albert Museum IS 38–1996). L. 83 cm, W. at base (front to back) 85 cm.

181 A young Kalash man of Rumbur Valley, Chitral, wearing the traditional men's trousers and shawl of his community, now rarely worn. The trousers (*dashak buth*) were given to Kalash boys at coming-of-age ceremonies: they are worn with the decorative edging and fringe turned over at the waist and hanging down like an apron.

who lived on both sides of the Afghan border. The Afghan Kafirs, living in Nuristan, were forcibly converted to Islam in the late nineteenth century, but the 3000-strong Kalash community still living in Pakistan have managed to retain their ancient traditions and religion. While the women still dress mainly in traditional Kalash style, the men have largely adopted the modern Pakistani dress of *shalwar kameez* instead of the woollen trousers (*dashak buth*; fig. 181) and jerkins that were formerly crucial to the various rites of passage ceremonies of the Kalash male. The traditional striped woollen cape of Kalash women of high rank (*jil*; fig. 183) and the plainer white woollen shawl (*charusti*) worn generally by women are still to be found, while the black cotton dress worn in milder weather is still in everyday use.

Another significant element of textile production in NWFP is felt-making. While often made in undecorated pieces for purposes such as tent-covering in various parts of Asia, felts (*namda*) made in Pakistan may be used as bedding (fig. 186), prayer rugs, floor-coverings (see fig. 184) or saddle-cloths, and are likely to have a simple geometric pattern in one or two

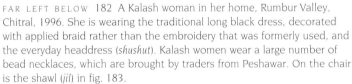

FAR LEFT BELOW 182 A Kalash woman in her home, Rumbur Valley, Chitral, 1996. She is wearing the traditional long black dress, decorated with applied braid rather than the embroidery that was formerly used, and the everyday headdress (*shushut*). Kalash women wear a large number of bead necklaces, which are brought by traders from Peshawar. On the chair is the shawl (*jil*) in fig. 183.

LEFT 183 Woollen shawl (*jil*) worn by high-ranking Kalash women, Rumbur Valley, Chitral (collection N. Askari). L. 112 cm, W. 125 cm. The shawl is made of two joined sections; a gap is left in the central seam, allowing the shawl to be worn over the head like an asymmetrical poncho.

ABOVE 184 Felt rug made in the Swat Valley, Mingora Bazaar, 1996. Felts with this type of design are used in Swat as bedding or floor-covers; others with a *mihrab* design are used as prayer rugs.

RIGHT ABOVE 185 Felt-maker laying out the pattern for a rug, near Miandam, Swat Valley, 1996. The coloured woollen strips that will form the design are laid out first; the large pile of carded wool for the main body of the rug will be spread out on top of the pattern, and the whole pile moistened and compressed to felt together.

RIGHT BELOW 186 Felt used as bedding on a *charpai* (string bed), Bahrain, Swat Valley, 1996

colours (see also p. 78 for felt made in Baluchistan). The pattern is laid out in strips of coloured wool on a reed mat (see fig. 185); the ginned or carded wool for the main field of the rug, which often remains undyed, is laid out in a large, fluffy pile on top. The whole mass is moistened, wrapped into a roll and beaten or trodden on until the fibres interlock to form a mat. Unlike many Central Asian forms of felt, those made in Swat are not stitched for either patterning or strengthening. The Swat Valley, especially the towns of Madyan and Bahrain, is the major felt-making area for NWFP, but felt can be found in small workshops all over the province and is reported to be made at Arandu, on the Afghan border close to the Chitral Valley, and formerly at Kohat, Bannu, Hazara and Dera Ghazi Khan.[4] Namdas from Azad Kashmir are usually embroidered with wool in elaborate chain-stitch patterns and are widely used as floor rugs and spreads.

Weaving in silk and cotton in NWFP has traditionally taken place in the urban centres of the southern parts of the province, such as Kohat, Peshawar and Bannu, although the Imperial Gazetteer of 1908 states that "coarse cotton fabrics are woven by hand in every part of the Province".[5] The elegant blue turban cloth from Rawalpindi (see fig. 143 in Punjab chapter) is typical of the fine cloths described in the same work.[6] The distinctive dark-blue cotton fabric with pink stripes used for trousers in NWFP, and particularly popular in Swat, is made at centres such as Chakwal in Punjab and imported into the province. Silk-weaving was carried out at Kohat and Peshawar, especially for silk turbans: Watt singles out a weaver called Gholam Hussein of Peshawar whose "beautiful goods" could be seen at the Delhi exhibition of 1903, together with those of one Abdul Jabbar of Kohat and lungi-weavers from the Punjab.[7] Impressive striped cotton turban-cloths with silk ends were also produced at Kohat,[8] and a distinctive shawl or curtain fabric with a dark-blue or black field and brightly coloured stripes of red, yellow and green silk at each end (see fig. 190) is still made today in Swat (although usually with synthetic ends). Beautiful shawls, also with dark-blue cotton central fields and brilliant silk bands and ends, were a speciality of Waziristan, on the Afghan border (fig. 189). Cotton fabric of high

187 Pair of women's trousers (shalwar), acquired from Dera Ghazi Khan in 1855 (Victoria and Albert Museum 05544 IS). Indigo-dyed cotton with pink silk stripes. L. 120 cm, W. at waist 400 cm. Immensely wide shalwar like these were commonly worn in NWFP until quite recently.

188 Woman's dress (khat), from Kohat, mid 19th century (Victoria and Albert Museum 4815 IS). Indigo-dyed cotton. L. 121 cm, W. at shoulders 37 cm. Plain blue cotton was frequently used for garments especially around Kohat and Bannu. A dress like this would be worn with wide, gathered cotton trousers (shalwar), with a plain shawl to cover the head.

quality to which Watt applies the all-purpose term of khes (see Punjab chapter) was also made in the area around Kohat and Peshawar,[9] and an indigo-dyed deep-blue cotton cloth produced there was "extensively used by both sexes in the valleys west of Kohat" (figs. 187, 188).[10]

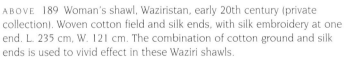

ABOVE 189 Woman's shawl, Waziristan, early 20th century (private collection). Woven cotton field and silk ends, with silk embroidery at one end. L. 235 cm, W. 121 cm. The combination of cotton ground and silk ends is used to vivid effect in these Waziri shawls.

ABOVE RIGHT 190 Part of a woven shawl, Swat, mid 19th century (Victoria and Albert Museum 7273 IS). Silk and cotton. Shawls with indigo-dyed cotton fields and striped silk ends in vivid colours are found in several parts of the Frontier area (see also figs. 189, 191). This particular colour combination is typical of Swat, although modern versions are less finely woven and more garish.

RIGHT 191 Woman's shawl, possibly from the Kaghan Valley, 20th century (Lamb Collection). Woven cotton field and silk end borders. L. 448 cm, W. 133 cm.

Embroidery The embroidered textiles of the North-West Frontier Province hint at a complex story of trade and migration, both within the Province itself and outside its boundaries, and of intermingling with the nomad peoples of Afghanistan and Central Asia

192 Woman's outer garment (*burqa*), probably from Waziristan, mid 20th century (*burqa*: collection F. Samee; *shalwar*: Victoria and Albert Museum 05595 IS). Magenta silk with gold-wire embroidery. The all-enveloping *burqa* is worn by Pathan women throughout NWFP. This is a particularly decorative version; *burqas* for everyday wear are usually in cotton or a synthetic equivalent, with a small amount of embroidery around the cap and front opening. They are often white, but more recently are also seen in deep, plain colours such as blue, purple or olive green. The *burqa* is shown here with a striped silk *shalwar*.

and the settled areas of the Punjab. Local styles of embroidery still survive in some areas of NWFP, mostly through women embroidering garments for their families, but in most places ready-made clothing has replaced the hand-made. The more isolated areas have retained their traditional embroidery styles, and the Kohistan region, stretching across the upper Swat and Indus Valleys, is a case in point. The people of this remote territory are ethnically distinct from the Pathan tribes of the western frontier and the settled areas of the Province: they belong to a relatively small group of what are sometimes called Dardic peoples (although this is a name given them by European ethnographers and not used locally) and which also includes the inhabitants of the territory stretching from Chitral across to Gilgit, Hunza and Baltistan.[11] Included within this diverse group of people are the Shin, the largest group, based around Gilgit and the valleys off the Indus, the Kho of Chitral and the Burusho of Hunza, each with their own languages and traditions. Outside this loose confederation of peoples, but living amongst them and sharing much of their culture, are the Gujars, travelling herdsmen who are to be found in hill country all over northern Pakistan and north India. The nomadic Powindahs, originally from Afghanistan, formerly crossed the border regularly on their yearly migrations, but their mobility has been severely restricted in recent years by stricter border controls.

Some of the finest embroidery of NWFP comes from the remote valleys of Indus Kohistan, especially the area between Patan and Kamila, where small settlements beside tributaries of the Indus – such as the Palas and Kolai Rivers – produce embroidered costume and small bags worked in minute cross stitch, surface darning stitch and tent stitch.[12] Almost no documentation exists for this extraordinarily fine work: it goes unremarked by commentators such as Watt, whose coverage of other areas is remarkably comprehensive. Until very recently the spectacular embroidered dresses of the area (*jumlo*; see fig. 193) were frequently sold by textile dealers even in nearby Peshawar as Nuristani (that is, from eastern Afghanistan). While these distinctive embroideries are now becoming recognized, it is in most cases too late to document their exact origins and local variations

ABOVE 193 Woman's dress (*jumlo*) from Indus Kohistan (collection N. Askari). Cotton with floss-silk embroidery, with buttons, beads and metal items. These extraordinary dresses are some of the most lavishly decorated costumes in Asia. Even the less elaborately embroidered examples always have the full skirt with multiple inserted panels: this example has 380 panels, others have been recorded with over 600.

LEFT 194 Woman's shawl from Indus Kohistan (Pip Rau Collection). Cotton with floss silk embroidery. L. 160 cm, W. 178 cm. The Kohistani shawls share the same fine embroidery as the dresses with which they are worn (see fig. 193). They are constructed of two overlapping embroidered panels, each with a beaded fringe, and the two corners are joined by turning up the lower edge. The join is usually embellished with a triangular beaded motif which, as well as being an auspicious emblem, adds weight to the bottom edge of the shawl.

as the elaborate traditional costumes are superseded by modern Pakistani dress.

In Indus Kohistan, costume is the vehicle for the finest embroidery. Most elaborately decorated are the dresses (*jumlo*) and the accompanying shawls (*chuprai*; figs. 194, 196), which are worn over trousers with finely embroidered cuffs (*paincha*). The Kohistani *jumlo* is a remarkable garment with wide sleeves and a full skirt into which are inserted a varying number of triangular panels – the dress illustrated in fig. 193 has an astonishing 380 panels in its skirt, and that in fig. 209 no fewer than 524.[13] The dress itself, in common with most other elements of the traditional costume, is made of a robust, often twill-woven, black cotton cloth bought in the local bazaar, and it is decorated on the front of the bodice and the sleeves. In the case of the most elaborate dresses, this decoration may cover almost the entire surface of these areas or, on less ambitious garments, it may be confined instead to the neck-opening and the cuffs. The *jumlo*, in common with other garments such as hats and waistcoats, is further adorned with coins, buttons of brass, mother-of-pearl or plastic; glass or plastic beads; amuletic motifs in metal or beadwork, and various dangling metal ornaments, often purpose-made. In more recent times, substitutions for the traditional decorations have appeared, such as key-ring chains, ring-pulls from soft drinks cans, and, most frequently, old zip-fasteners used as decorative edgings. The embroidery itself is of two main types, both of which are very frequently used on the same garment (see detail of fig. 194): a tiny cross stitch, often worked in patterns of minute squares, and a longer darning stitch akin to that of the *phulkari* of the Hazara district (see figs. 201, 203). On the *jumlo*, the cross stitch is usually seen on the area around the neck-opening and in narrow borders between areas of larger motifs, while the surface darning stitch is used for the large serrated roundels that are often used on the front and shoulders, and are also found in the branching patterns on children's hats (see fig. 196) and, less

Detail of fig. 194, showing the two main embroidery stitches used in Indus Kohistan: the darning stitch used in the larger 'ram's horn' motif and the cross stitch of the border pattern.

195 Woman's shawl from Indus Kohistan (Victoria and Albert Museum IS 2-1997). Cotton with floss-silk embroidery, sequins, mirrors and beads. L. 146 cm, W. 204 cm. Although less fine and less old than the piece in fig. 194, the design of this shawl uses the same format on a somewhat larger scale.

frequently, waistcoats. Where the waistcoats are patterned with a square-based design, the embroidery may be almost entirely in cross stitch (figs. 197, 198). Other small objects, such as trouser-cuffs, gun-covers and tobacco pouches (kochor) are also embroidered all over their surfaces with exquisite cross-, tent- and satin-stitch embroidery (see fig. 199). It is worth noting that similar small items embroidered all over with the same stitches are made by the Uzbeks of northern Afghanistan and Hazaras in central Afghanistan,[14] although no detailed work has yet been done on the possible interrelationship between these areas and Kohistan. The Hazara work in particular seems remarkably close in design as well as technique to that of Indus Kohistan, with patterns of interlocking rhomboids, a dominant feature in both traditions. In the Palas Valley in Indus Kohistan, a branching motif is embroidered in chain stitch (see fig. 200) to decorate women's and children's gar-

ments and utilitarian objects such as gun-covers. The chain stitch is worked on quite a large scale and is therefore much less time-consuming than the minute embroidery stitches traditionally used in the area; it may have been taken up as an easier alternative. It perhaps derives from the woollen chain stitch embroidery used on decorated coats (see fig. 179).

The use of a *phulkari*-type stitch in this remote northern area is a reminder of the continuous and far-reaching movement that has traditionally taken place both within the Kohistan region itself and between Kohistan and the Punjab and Hazara districts. It is evident both from documentation of observers such as John Biddulph (1880) and from the fact that there appears to have been continuous movement between all these areas of materials (for example, beads), patterns (especially the borders of the shawls) and techniques (such as satin/darning stitch) that there was considerable contact between

196 Child's hat from Indus Kohistan (Pip Rau Collection). Cotton, embroidered with floss silk and embellished with beads, buttons, shells and zip-fasteners. H. 56 cm, W. at bottom 56 cm. This elaborate headgear is now rarely seen in Indus Kohistan, but smaller versions with sparser embroidery are still in use.

197 A child wearing an embroidered waistcoat made by her mother, Kuzkili village, Kolai Valley, Indus Kohistan, 1996

198 Child's waistcoat from Indus Kohistan (Victoria and Albert Museum IS 32-1996). Cotton embroidered with silk, with buttons, beads, and zip-fasteners. L. 40 cm, W. 37.5 cm. The embroidery on this small jacket is done entirely in minute cross-stitches.

Reverse of fig. 198

199 Two tobacco pouches from Indus Kohistan, probably Kolai or Palas Valley (collection S.J. Cohen). Cotton embroidered with silk. (Left) L. 19 cm, W. 19 cm; (right) L. 15 cm, W. 14 cm. The beaded loop on the side of the bag was used to hang it from the *huqqa* (water-pipe) while it was being smoked.

200 Woman's shirt from Indus Kohistan (Victoria and Albert Museum IS 3-1997). Cotton embroidered with silk, with coins, buttons, sequins and metal ornaments. L. 98 cm, W. 156 cm. The decoration on this shirt is quite different in style from the more densely embroidered garments in figs. 193–199, although it is from the same area. The chain stitch is not usual in traditional embroidery from Indus Kohistan, and this design may be a later addition to the repertoire of the area.

201 Woman's embroidered shawl from Hazara (collection N. Askari). L. 226 cm, W. 109 cm. This type of Hazara embroidery is quite distinct from the *phulkari* tradition of the area, and is usually done in shades of pink on a black or white ground. The designs (see detail opposite) incorporate 'star' and 'ram's horn' patterns.

202 Woman's shawl (*chadar*), Swat Valley, late 19th to early 20th century (Lamb Collection). Cotton embroidered with floss silk. L. 247 cm, W. 100 cm. The dense red silk embroidery of the end borders of this shawl use the typical 'ram's horn' pattern seen not only in Swat but also in many parts of Central Asia. The diamond shapes found in Hazara *phulkari* embroidery are also used in the area around the central medallion.

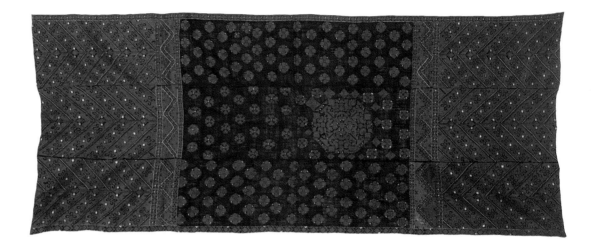

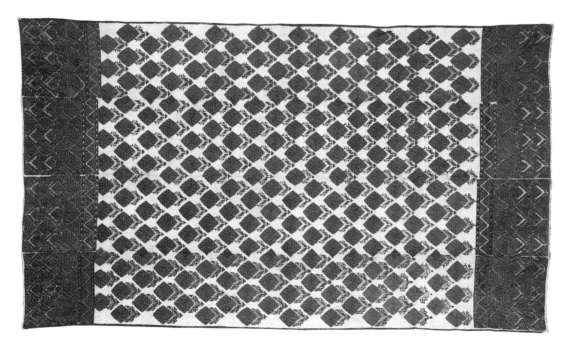

203 Woman's shawl from Hazara (Lamb Collection). Cotton embroidered with silk. L. 258 cm, W. 146 cm. The floss silk embroidery of the Hazara region obviously has close links with that of the Punjab (see fig. 158), both in terms of design and technique, but the Hazara *phulkari* tend to use a wider range of colours and less rigidly geometric designs.

FACING PAGE Detail of fig. 201

LEFT Detail of fig. 203

RIGHT 204 Woman's shawl (*chadar*), Swat Valley, early 20th century (Lamb Collection). Cotton embroidered with floss silk. L. 260 cm, W. 135 cm. This is an unusually ornate example of the fine silk embroidery done in the Swat Valley. While it has similarities with the *phulkari* of Hazara and the Punjab, the designs used here are much more complex than the simple geometric shapes often found in those embroideries.

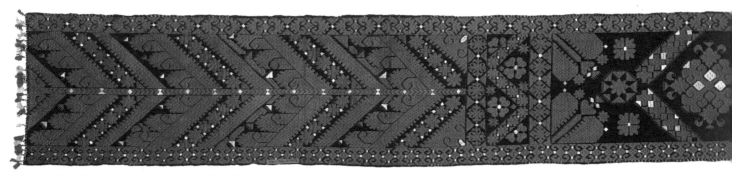

205 Man's embroidered wedding turban from the Swat Valley (Lamb Collection). L. 378 cm, W. 38.5 cm. The elaborate embroidery on this long, indigo-dyed cotton turban is worked on both sides to a remarkable thickness. This is a particularly lavish example of a traditional Swati turban type: some are decorated only at the ends.

206 Woman's embroidered shirt (*kurta*) from the Swat Valley (Victoria and Albert Museum IS 92-1963). Indigo-dyed cotton with pink floss-silk embroidery. L. 82 cm, W. 133 cm.

This *kurta* combines the scattered geometric motifs of fig. 207 with the more solid blocks of embroidery seen in the Swati shawls and turbans of figs. 204 and 205.

Indus/Swat Kohistan and neighbouring areas in all directions. This includes northwards into Central Asia: the geometric designs of certain Kohistani embroideries (see fig. 194) are undeniably similar to the *gul* motifs found, for example, in Turkmen rugs.[15] It is also significant that there is an oral tradition of earlier migrations from Swat to Indus Kohistan,[16] and of the inhabitants of upper Swat having been forced northwards by Pathan harrassment.[17] There has always been a close connection between the Swat and Indus Valleys, connected as they are by the Kandia Valley in the north and the Shangla Pass in the south. It is only in living memory that inhabitants of Indus Kohistan have stopped going to the main market in Swat to buy luxuries such as glass beads (*shong*) for embroi-dery – a journey that took four days on foot in each direction.[18]

The surface darning-stitch embroidery used in Indus Kohistan is almost always employed either as roundels with feathered or serrated edges or as border designs with branched or 'ram's horn' designs along the edges of shawls and garments (see fig. 194). Sometimes the fine workmanship of a more elaborate border suggests that it might have been embroidered in the Hazara district and attached to a main section embroidered in Indus Kohistan, just as the broad embroidered cuffs of some *jumlos* appear to have been purchased separately and attached. The availability in the markets of Swat of embroidered panels for dresses and hats from Indus Kohistan confirms

207 Woman's embroidered shirt (*kurta*), Swat Valley, early 20th century (collection N. Askari). L. 81 cm, W. 135 cm. The indigo-dyed cotton field and the use of a single shade of bright pink geometric embroidery are typical features of Swat Valley embroidery and are common to *kurtas* and shawls. This *kurta* has bands of exceptionally fine embroidery at each shoulder.

that embroideries from other parts of the region could be purchased and attached to garments far from their place of origin.

In contrast to Indus Kohistan with its fondness for tiny cross-stitch designs, the Swat Valley and its lower-lying neighbour Hazara are traditionally associated with embroidery of the *phulkari* type. The close link with the *phulkari* of neighbouring Punjab is most clearly seen in the embroidered shawls of Hazara (fig. 203), which use diamond and chevron patterns that are closely comparable to those of the Punjabi *chadars* (see fig. 158). The Hazara pieces, however, typically use a colour scheme of dark pink on a white or dark-blue ground, in contrast to the yellow and orange of the Punjab, and the design elements themselves

often have a 'feathered' effect on the outlines unlike the straight edges seen in the Punjabi pieces. Hazara is also the source of another distinctive type of white-ground shawl with pink and red designs in a markedly different style from the *phulkari* (see fig. 201), with curling horned and star patterns.

While it is frequently difficult to determine whether *phulkari* embroideries were made in Hazara or in neighbouring Swat, the style of embroidery from Swat tends, both in design and technique, to be further removed from the simpler *phulkari* styles than embroidery from Hazara. The lavishly embroidered textiles associated with weddings in Swat – shawls, turbans, cushion-covers – are heavily embroidered with floss silk, sometimes on both sides of the cloth (figs. 204,

ABOVE 210 A pair of wooden shoes from Swat (private collection). H. 7 cm, L. 25 cm. These pattens, designed to raise the wearer above the muddy streets, are carved with designs similar to those with which the Swati craftsmen decorated the furniture and architecture of the area.

BELOW 211 Carving on the doorway of the main mosque in Kalam, Upper Swat Valley. Swat is known for its intricate wood-carving, traditionally used on architecture and furniture, as well as smaller items such as shoes (see above), boxes and Quran-stands.

LEFT ABOVE 208 Woman's dress, Swat Valley or Swat Kohistan, *ca.* 1880 (Victoria and Albert Museum 1830-1883 IS). Cotton embroidered with floss silk. L. 92 cm, W. across sleeves 188 cm. This unusual garment has strong similarities with the embroidered *kurtas* of Swat, where it was acquired in 1881–82, but the arrangement of embroidery, especially on the sleeves, suggests a link with Kohistan.

LEFT BELOW 209 Woman's dress (*jumlo*), Swat Kohistan (Victoria and Albert Museum IS 33-1996). Cotton embroidered with silk. H. 90 cm, W. across sleeves 182 cm. This dress is in the Indus Kohistan style (see fig. 193) but the embroidery is quite different: apart from the added cuffs which are done in cross stitch, all the embroidery is in a surface darn stitch like the Swati shawls and *kurtas*. The gored skirt has 524 panels.

205, 212), and frequently with such dense patterns that the ground cloth is scarcely visible. The Swat *phulkaris* may be embroidered from the front, unlike the Punjabi type in which the embroidery is always done from the back of the cloth, and the patterns may first be outlined with running stitch before being filled in with satin stitch. The women's shirts (*kurta*) that were once widely worn in Swat are embroidered with pink floss silk on dark-blue indigo-dyed cotton. The embroidery on these *kurtas* varies from small, scattered *phulkari*-type medallions (see fig. 207) to thickly embroidered panels of solid embroidery (fig. 206).[19] The back of the *kurta* is usually left undecorated.

Closer to the Kohistan style of geometric cross-stitch embroidery is a type of small-scale work common to both Hunza and Chitral. Mostly confined to women's circular caps (see figs. 217, 218) and other small items such as purses and belts, the embroidery of Hunza in particular can be extremely fine. Patterns are usually geometric and are worked in tiny cross stitch, or today only half-cross stitch. The same type of embroidery is found in Chitral, perhaps having been introduced from Hunza, and is used for similar objects: caps (very similar to the Hunza style, but usually with less deep brims), detachable cuffs and collars, and small bags (see figs. 219, 220). These small embroidered objects are called *suru* and are often found as dowry items.[20] While they share similar geometric patterns with the Hunza embroideries, the Chitrali embroiderers seem to favour more garish colours, especially purple and bright green.

Embroidery is also a feature of the Kalash women's costume, in which the voluminous black robes are embroidered with orange and yellow braids around the neck and cuffs. The elaborate Kalash ceremonial headdress, the *kupas*, which is strikingly similar in form and decoration to the turquoise-covered headdress of Ladakhi women, is made of wool lavishly embroidered with rows of cowrie shells and with medallions of brass, shells, buttons and metal *grelots* at the lower end (see fig. 223). This is also usually decorated with a simple woven geometric design similar to that used on the waistband of the *dashak buth* trousers and on the ends of the women's shawls (*charusti*). Under the *kupas*, or on its own for everyday

ABOVE 212 Pillow-cover, Swat Valley, 20th century (Lamb Collection). Cotton embroidered with floss silk, with woollen braiding and tassels added later. L. 95 cm, W. 49 cm. The indigo-dyed ground fabric is hardly visible through the dense embroidery of this pillow-cover, which would have been made for a wedding.

LEFT 213 Coverlet, Madyan, Swat Valley, *ca.* 1930 (Victoria and Albert Museum IM 37-1938; gift of Major E.H. Cobb, Political Agent, Dir Swat and Chitral). Cotton embroidered with silk. L. 71 cm, W. 71.5 cm. The striking geometric design of this piece links it unmistakeably to Central Asian embroidery, with its border of 'ram's horn' motifs doubling as human figures and branching-tree motifs in the field. The dark-blue/black and pink colour scheme is typical of Swat, as are the *phulkari* medallions almost hidden in the main pattern.

use, a *shushut* is worn, a circlet of woollen cloth embroidered with red and yellow braids and decorated with cowrie shells or buttons, which has a similarly decorated tail that hangs down the back (see figs. 182, 221, 222).[21] The female costume is completed by many red-bead necklaces, which are acquired from traders from Peshawar who exchange the beads for local walnuts, each one costing six walnuts.

214 Woman's tunic, made by Mangalli nomads in Pakistan, early 20th century (collection H. Iwatate). Cotton embroidered with silk. Although the Mangalli are usually associated with Afghanistan, the embroidery added to the lower part of this tunic strongly suggests a Pakistani origin.

215 Woman's dress probably from the Dera Ismail Khan region, mid 19th century (Victoria and Albert Museum 05488 IS). Embroidered cotton. L. 120.5 cm, W. across shoulders 43 cm. The bodice of this dress is decorated with drawn-thread work as well as simple embroidery in coloured silks. The reverse of the bodice has a squared pattern.

TOP LEFT 217 A Hunza woman wearing an embroidered cap, Hunza, 1996. The head-cover is normally worn over the cap.

TOP RIGHT 218 Three embroidered women's caps from Hunza (collection F.S. Aijazuddin (left and top) and private collection (right)). Left: H. 6 cm, diam. 19 cm; top: H. 6 cm, diam. 17.5 cm; right: H. 8 cm, diam.18 cm. The fine embroidery of the Hunza Valley is done in silk cross stitch on a cotton ground.

BELOW LEFT 220 Embroidered headbands, a purse and a holder for a *kohl* container from Chitral, *ca*. 1930 (Victoria and Albert Museum IM 45- to 49-1938; gift of Major E.H. Cobb). Top: W. 5 cm, L. 50 cm; below: W. 6 cm, L. 53 cm; bottom left: H. 9 cm, W. 10.5 cm; bottom right: H. 10 cm, W. 3.5 cm. The fine cross-stitch of the Chitrali embroidery, as well as the geometric and leaf designs, show close links with that of Hunza (see fig. 218), and may have been introduced to Chitral from there.

BELOW RIGHT 219 Small bag, probably from Hunza (collection N. Askari). Cotton embroidered with silk. L. 34 cm, W. 24 cm.

LEFT 216 Woman's dress, Waziristan, early 20th century (Victoria and Albert Museum IS 39-1996). Cotton embroidered with floss silk. L. 102 cm. This remarkable style combines elements from several parts of NWFP and neighbouring Afghanistan.The *phulkari*-type medallions recall the embroideries of Swat and Hazara, while the bands of embroidery on the sleeves and the triangular inserts into the skirt suggest contact with Indus Kohistan. The intricately braided decoration on the neck is close to the type used by the Mangalli nomads of western Afghanistan, who were traditionally also to be found on the Pakistan side of the border (see fig. 214).

221 A Kalash woman wearing the everyday headdress, the *shushut*, Birir Valley, Chitral, 1996. The long 'tail' of the *shushut* is thought to have evolved from long, loose fringes. This woman is making a cotton sash (*shuman*) by finger-weaving.

222 A Kalash girl, Rumbur Valley, Chitral, 1996. Girls wear exactly the same as the adults. The hair-style with the front plait is traditional amongst Kalash women.

223 A Kalash woman wearing the ceremonial headdress, *kupas*, Birir Valley, Chitral, 1996. The *kupas* is normally worn only at festivals, when it is placed on top of the longer *shushut*, as here. This *kupas* was made entirely by its owner.

Block-Printing and Roghan Block-printing is carried out all over Pakistan and, while its best known centres are in Punjab and Sindh, NWFP is no exception. Cotton fabric is block-printed with simple patterns for furnishings and for women's garments at Swabi in Mardan district and Haripur in Hazara.[22] More distinctive than block-printed cotton, however, is the *roghan* or 'wax-cloth' work particularly associated with Peshawar, in which cotton or silk cloth is decorated by applying a soft, wax-like substance (*roghan*) produced from the oil of the safflower seed (see fig. 40). Pigments such as orpiment and red lead are added to the *roghan*,[23] and the ductile substance is manipulated on to the surface of the cloth by a metal pointer. The process has been likened to "drawing a pattern in thick treacle by means of a skewer",[24] but in spite of this unwieldy technique, surprisingly fine lines and designs are produced by manipulating the soft gum on the surface of the fabric with a moistened fingertip. A silvery effect is sometimes obtained by dusting the *roghan* with powdered mica. The *roghan* technique is traditionally associated with the Afridi tribe of Pathans, who live in the area around Peshawar and Kohat, and this type of cloth was formerly made commercially in Peshawar.[25] It could be used for garments as well as for furnishings,[26] but is perhaps better suited to large-scale patterns, and became popular with European customers for hangings.

RIGHT 224 A *roghan*-work hanging or prayer mat from Peshawar, *ca.* 1890 (Victoria and Albert Museum IS 19-1894). H. 145 cm, W. 91.5 cm. The design on this hanging is produced by trailing a waxy substance made from safflower oil dyed with pigments on to the surface of the cloth.

Notes

INTRODUCTION

1. Jarrige, p. 211 and fig. 4.5.

2. *Ibid.*, p. 248.

3. There are only a small number of sites outside South Asia that provide earlier evidence for textile production than at Mehrgarh: the earliest is the Neolithic site at Jarmo in North-East Iraq, where impressions of plain-weave and basket-weave textiles have been left in clay (Barber, pp. 126–27). These impressions are datable to about 7000 BC.

4. Wheeler, p. 63.

5. See Gittinger, pp. 15–16.

6. See for example Agrawala, who quotes Panini (*ca.* fifth century BC) as listing silk, linen, woollen and cotton textiles (pp. 125–26; pp. 231–34). Panini also mentions the dye-stuffs madder (*manjistha*) and indigo (*nili*) (*ibidem*, p. 209).

7. Burton, p. 61.

8. Blochmann, p. 57.

9. See for example Walker, p. 255.

10. See for example *Indian Heritage* nos. 198, 199.

11. Blochmann, p. 98: A'*in* 32, 'On shawls, stuffs, etc.'.

12. See Irwin, *passim*.

13. Irwin and Schwarz, p. 20.

14. Foster, 1624–29, p. 93.

15. Irwin and Schwarz, p. 12.

16. Foster, loc. cit.

17. Foster, 1634–36, p. 130.

18. Foster, 1642–45, p. 309; 1646–50, p. 152.

19. Linschoten, I, pp. 56 and 382.

20. Manrique, chap. LXX.

21. India Office Library, London, Letter Book IX, p. 410.

22. Watt, p. 377.

23. *Ibid.*, p. 390.

SINDH

1. Historically, Tharr, implying desert or sand hills, was known as the Little Desert (also Dhat or Thal) as it referred to a strip of desert along the northern border of the Rann of Kutch which together with western Rajasthan made up the Great Desert.

Parkar, south-east of Tharr was a promontory jutting out into the Rann of Kutch and made up of rocky hills. See Raikes, p. 2.

2. This shawl is referred to as an *odhani*, *bugh* or *chunari* (often shortened to *chunni*) depending on the nature of its decoration, *i.e.* embroidery, block-print or tie-dye, and as a *pothi* when it is made of lightweight red cotton and worn covering the head (personal communication, Nawaz Ali Khan, Nagarparkar, February 1994).

3. The Rajputs (lit. 'sons of kings' or *rajahs*) entered the subcontinent from the north west and established kingdoms in western India, which today make up the states of Rajasthan, Gujarat, Madhya Pradesh and the south eastern areas of Sindh.

4. The *phulhri* ('bud') stitch is found in a number of Sindhi embroideries but its use in women's shawls from Tharparkar is very distinctive. When densely compacted together the stitches are popularly referred to as the *dandhtaka* ('toothed stitch'). See also Watt, p. 391.

5. For a fascinating account of dowry clothes of related groups who live on the borders of Tharparkar and Kutch, see Elson, pp. 69–89.

6. Rabari legends relate that they took to wearing black garments in the fifteenth century to mourn the death of their ruler.

7. Throughout Sindh the history of group migration relies on oral tradition. It is generally agreed that the Jats were cattle breeders and herders who travelled from an area between modern-day Iran and Iraq some eight centuries ago in search of pasture. Over the years this quest led them further afield, through Iran and parts of Afghanistan down to Sindh, Kutch and Gujarat. For a more comprehensive account of their origins see Westphal-Hellbusch and Westphal, pp. 13–51.

8. The hurmitch or interlacing stitch is characteristic of central Sindh but is now found in embroideries all over Sindh. A lattice of stitches is put on the surface of a fabric, into which threads are then interwoven.

9. Martin, p. 36.

10. Burton 1973, p. 301.

11. *Zardozi* is a word of Persian origin literally translated as 'gold stitching' (Persian *zar*: 'gold'). This art enjoyed great patronage under the Mughals and in adjoining Rajput kingdoms, and continues up to the present day. Specialized methods were used

to draw out, flatten, plait, spin and twist gold and silver wires in order to achieve distinctive effects in the embroidery. See N.A. Baloch, p. 41.

12. Birdwood, p. 69.

13. Aitken, p. 390.

14. *Ibid.*, p. 393.

15. *Ibid.*

16. Duarte 1974, p. 23.

17. Brendon, p. 12.

18. Hughes, p. 319.

19. Aitken, pp. 394–95.

20. Cousin, p. 78.

21. *Ibid.*; see also Varadarajan.

BALUCHISTAN

1. Field, p. 12.

2. Buller, p. 27. The Meds continue to live in the coastal areas, the Afghans beyond the Takht-e-Sulaiman and the Jats are the principal farming groups of Las Bela and Kach.

3. This may have been a legacy of the Persian frock coat and trousers (Nawab Akbar Khan Bugti, personal communication, 1996).

4. Among the Brahvis the pocket is also referred to as a *jaib* or *gubtaan*. It usually has a triangular top section, the tip of which is attached to the lower edge of the yoke.

5. *Shalwar* often have embroidered cuffs at the ankles. Brightly covered *kanavez* cloth was probably brought in from Herat.

6. The braids are popularly called *shiraz*, and are card-woven.

7. Pottinger, p. 28.

8. *Ibid.*, p. 18. "An *Ulkhaliq* is a double breasted dress with long sleeves, and to sit to the form as low as the hips, and having skirts reaching down to the calf of the leg; it is tied across the chest on the left side. *Keemkhwab* is a species of silk, with gold or silver sprigs or flowers worked on it." An *ulkhaliq* is also used to describe a chintz tunic lined and stuffed with cotton.

9. Because of their reliance on sheep, the Brahvi have a pithy saying, 'God is great, but a sheep is a different thing.'

PUNJAB

1. Kipling 1888, p. 69.

2. *Ibid.*, p. 57.

3. *Ibid.*, p. 69.

4. *Ibid.*, p. 68.

5. Forbes Watson, First Series, 1867,

nos. 102–27.

6. Jamil, pp. 85–86; Gardezi, pp. 72–76.

7. *Ibid.*, p. 74.

8. *Ibid.*, pp. 76–77.

9. See Cohen, *passim*.

10. *Ibid.*, pp. 16–17, fig. 13.

11. Cookson, p. 70. "At no time does the cultivation of the silkworm seem to have been carried on systematically by the natives of the Province. Where sericulture has existed at all, it has been taken up rather as a means of adding a few rupees to the income of the household … than as an earnest means of livelihood. Efforts have been made from time to time by European gentlemen to establish the industry on a firmer footing; but the success achieved has been very small."

12. Gardezi, pp. 79–83.

13. For illustrations of *ezarband* weaving, see Yacopino, p. 50, and Hailey, fig. 9j (discussion on p. 15).

14. See Kipling 1888, p. 31.

15. *Ibid.*, p. 58.

16. See Brown, p. 91; Watt, p. 429.

17. See Yacopino, p. 122.

18. There are many differing traditions relating to the giving and use of *phulkari*. See for example Hailey, p. 16: "The slightest difference in pattern [of the *phulkari*] seems to warrant a change in nomenclature. The *bund* is worn as a covering by a bride on the first day of her marriage; the *sirga* is given by the bride's relations to the elderly persons present at the marriage." Yacopino, p. 42: "In villages in the northern Punjab the wedding *phulkari* is embroidered by the bridegroom's family. Before the bridegroom leaves his home for the marriage ceremony, he takes a bath and the *phulkari* is held over his head as a canopy by four relatives. The groom drapes the *phulkari* over his shoulders during the wedding procession to the bride's home where he then ceremoniously presents it to her." Nabholz-Kartaschoff, p. 190: "Women used to wear a *bagh* during the annual fasting for their husbands or after the birth of their first son. *Bagh* were also hung up as decorations for festivals, or the arrival of honoured guests and presented to temples as gifts."

19. Flora Annie Steel, one of the first writers on *phulkari* embroidery, holds that it is originally a product of Hindu Jat (farming) society (Steel, p. 71) and spread according to their movements within the Punjab.

20. Acacia bark may also be used. See 'Phulkari' by E. Ledward, in Sandhu, p. 31.

21. Different colours of both ground fabric and embroidery silk, as well as different designs, were used in the Hazara *phulkari*: see NWFP chapter.

22. See for example *Costumes of Royal India*, pls. 1, 10, 59, 65.

23. See Murphy, p. 19.

24. Kipling (1888, p. 69) also mentions the town of Talamba, not far from Kamalia, as another source of good cotton prints.

25. Kipling 1886, p. 104.

26. Watt, p. 244.

27. *Ibid.*, p. 246.

NORTH-WEST FRONTIER PROVINCE

1. Singh and Ahivasi, p. 1.

2. This recalls the usage of the felt coats of Badakhshan in Afghanistan, which often have unusable sleeves which are designed to hang from the wearer's shoulders (see Burkett, pls. 26 and 27). Coats of woven fabric with long sleeves that are not intended to have the arms inserted are also found among the Turkmen and Uzbeks of Central Asia.

3. See for example Burkett, cat. nos. 47, 50.

4. Watt, p. 341; *Imperial Gazetteer of India, North-West Frontier Province*, p. 50.

5. *Ibid.*

6. *Ibid.*: "Finer fabrics are generally woven for *lungis* (turbans), mostly in grey or dark blue, with richly worked end-pieces in bands of gold thread (*tila*) or coloured silk."

7. Watt, p. 301.

8. *Imperial Gazetteer*, loc. cit.; Watt, pp. 301–02.

9. Watt, p. 274.

10. See Forbes Watson, Third Series, 1867, nos. 97 and 99.

11. See for example Kalter, p. 171.

12. Surface darning stitch has the appearance (from the front) of satin stitch, with the distinction that satin-stitch embroidery is equally visible on the reverse of the fabric, whereas in surface darn stitch the main pattern is seen only on the front, with the outline visible in tiny stitches on the reverse.

13. Paine 1994 mentions one dress with 674 panels (p. 52).

14. See for example Harvey, illus. 180, 183, 188–89, 195–99. The Hazara are a community of Mongol

origin who live in central Afghanistan. The fact that the Hazara region of Pakistan bears the same name appears to be coincidental and is perhaps due to a possible origin in the Persian *hazar* 'thousand'.

15. See Harvey, p. 45, for an example.

16. See Biddulph, pp. 7 and 8.

17. *Ibid.*, p. 69.

18. Personal communication from Sarbuland Khan, Kolai Valley, who now buys such items at the market in nearby Dubair. See also Barth, p. 27

19. See Kalter, figs. 101–04, for a group of embroidered *kurtas* with widely varying patterns.

20. Aseer, p. 206.

21. Sperber's excellent article on Kalash dress describes the development of the 'tail' of the *shushut* from loose fringes to the long, broad woven strip that is now common. The same article also gives valuable information on the use and manufacture of the *kupas*, the various types of shawl, and the other items of Kalash clothing.

22. Yacopino, p. 82, also mentions Badaber in Peshawar District as a block-printing centre.

23. Brown, p. 117.

24. *Ibid.*

25. A similar technique has been recorded from parts of Gujarat in India, possibly practised by descendants of Pathan immigrants (Watt, p. 233).

26. A dress in the British Museum presumably made for an Afridi woman combines *roghan* work with embroidery (1966.1.612); a woman's shawl in the Victoria and Albert acquired in Swat is decorated all over with brilliant pink patterns in the style of Swati embroidery (IM 43-1938).

Select Bibliography

Agrawala, V.S., *India as known to Panini*, London 1953

Aitken, E.H., *Gazetteer of the Province of Sind*, Karachi 1907

Alaudin, M., *Kalash: The Paradise Lost*, Lahore 1992

Aseer, Sher Wali Khan, 'The Marriage of Daughters in Chitral', *Proceedings of the Second International Hindukush Cultural Conference*, edd. E. Bashir and Israr-ud-Din, Karachi 1996

Auj, N.Z.A., *Legacy of Cholistan*, Multan 1995

Baloch, L.A.S., *Thur: The Cradle of a Great and Flourishing Civilisation* [unpublished manuscript], Hyderabad 1991

Baloch, M.S.K., *History of the Baluch Race and Baluchistan*, Karachi 1958

Baloch, N.A. (ed.), *The Traditional Arts and Crafts of the Hyderabad Region*, Hyderabad 1966

Barber, E.J.W., *Prehistoric Textiles: The Development of Cloth in the Neolithic and Bronze Ages*, Princeton 1991

Barth, F., *Indus and Swat Kohistan, an ethnographic survey*, Oslo 1956

Bashir, E. and Israr-ud-Din (edd.), *Proceedings of the Second International Hindukush Cultural Conference*, Karachi 1996

Bhushan, J.B., *The Costumes and Textiles of India*, Delhi 1958

Biddulph, J., *Tribes of the Hindoo Koosh* [Calcutta 1880], repr. Karachi 1973

Bilgrami, N., *Sindh jo Ajrak*, Karachi 1990

Birdwood, G.S.L., *The Industrial Arts of India*, London 1880

Black, D. and C. Loveless, *Rugs of the Wandering Baluchi*, London 1976

Blochmann, H. (trans.), *The A'in-i Akbari*, 3rd edn., New Delhi 1977

Bray, Sir D., *The Life History of a Brahui*, London 1913

Brendon, B.A., *A Monograph on the Woollen Fabrics of the Bombay Presidency*, Bombay 1899

Brown, P., *Lahore Museum, Punjab: A Descriptive Guide*, Lahore 1909

Bühler, A., *Ikat Batik Plangi*, Basle 1972

Buller, H.R., *Imperial Gazetteer of Baluchistan*, London 1908

Bunting, E.J., *Sindhi Tombs and Textiles*, Albuquerque 1980

Burkett, M.E., *The Art of the Felt Maker*, Kendal 1979

Burnes, A., *Travels into Bukhara and a Voyage on the Indus*, London 1834

Burton, R.F., *Sind and the Races that inhabit the Valley of the Indus*, repr. Karachi 1973

—— *Sind Revisited*, repr. Karachi 1993

Cohen, S., *The Unappreciated Dhurrie*, London 1982

Cookson, H.C., 'Monograph on the Silk Industry of the Punjab, 1886–7', *Journal of Indian Art*, ii, no. 24, 1888

Costumes of Royal India, Tokyo 1988

Cousin, F., 'Lumière et ombre, bleu et rouge: les azrak du Sind', *Objets et Mondes*, XVI, 1976

Dani, A.H., *Indus Civilisation – New Perspectives*, Islamabad 1981

Dhamija, J. and J. Jain (edd.), *Handwoven Fabrics of India*, Ahmedabad 1989

Duarte, A., *The Beggar Saint of Sehwan and Other Sketches of Sind*, Karachi 1974

—— *The Crafts and Textiles of Sind and Baluchistan*, Jamshoro 1982

Edwards, S.M., *A Monograph upon the Silk Fabrics of the Bombay Presidency*, Bombay 1900

Einthoven, R.E., *The Cotton Fabrics of the Bombay Presidency*, Bombay 1900

Elson, V., *Dowries from Kutch: A Women's Folk Art Tradition in India*, Los Angeles 1979

Fawcett, C.G.H., *A Monograph on Dyes and Dyeing in the Bombay Presidency*, Bombay 1896

Field, H., *An Anthropological Reconnaissance in West Pakistan*, Massachusetts 1959

Fisher, N. (ed.), *Mud, Mirror and Thread: Folk Traditions of Rural India*, Santa Fe and Ahmedabad 1993

Forbes Watson, J., *The Textile Manufactures and the Costumes of the People of India*, London 1867

—— *The Textile Fabrics of India* (sample books, 18 vols.), London 1867

—— *Collection of Specimens and Illustrations of the Textile Manufactures of India* (Second Series), London 1873

—— *Illustrations of the Textile Manufactures of India*, London 1881

Foster, W., *The English Factories in India, 1618–1699*, 13 vols., Oxford 1906–27

Frater, J., *Threads of Identity: Embroidery and Adornment of the Nomadic Rabaris*, Ahmedabad 1995

—— 'The Meaning of Folk Art in Rabari Life: A Closer Look at Mirrored Embroideries', *Textile Museum Journal*, iv, no. 2, 1975

Beg, M.K.F. (trans.), *Chachnama: An Ancient History of Sind*, Karachi 1900

Gardezi, H., *Crafts of the Punjab, III: Bhera*, Lahore 1993

Gittinger, M., *Master Dyers to the World. Technique and Trade in Early Indian Dyed Cotton Textiles*, Washington 1982

Grant, A.J., 'The Leather Industry of the Punjab', *Journal of Indian Art*, vii, no. 54, 1896

Hailey, W.M., 'Silk Industry in the Punjab', *Journal of Indian Art*, x, no. 81, 1903

Harvey, J., *Traditional Textiles of Central Asia*, London 1996

Hughes, A.W., *Gazetteer of the Province of Sind*, London 1876

Imperial Gazetteer of India [Oxford 1908], repr. (Provincial Series) Lahore 1991

London, Victoria and Albert Museum, *The Indian Heritage: Court Life and Arts under Mughal Rule*, 1982

Irwin, J.C., *The Girdlers Carpet*, London 1962

—— and M. Hall, *Indian Painted and Printed Fabrics*, Ahmedabad 1971

—— and —— *Indian Embroideries*, Ahmedabad 1973

—— and P. Schwarz, *Studies in Indo-European Textile History*, Ahmedabad 1966

Jamil, T., *Crafts of the Punjab, II: Multan*, Lahore 1988

Janmahmad, M., *The Baluch Cultural Heritage*, Karachi 1982

Jansen, M., M. Mulloy and G. Urgan (edd.), *Forgotten Cities on the Indus*, Mainz 1991

Jarrige, C. et al. (edd.), *Mehrgarh. Field Reports 1974–1985: From Neolithic Times to the Indus Civilization*, Karachi [1995–96]

Kalter, J., *The Arts and Crafts of the Swat Valley: Living Traditions in the Hindu Kush*, London 1991

Khuhro, Hamida (ed.), *Sind through the Centuries*, Karachi 1981

Khurshid, Z., 'Phulkaris: The Catalogue of Specimens in the Collection of the Lahore Museum', *Lahore Museum Bulletin*, v, no. 2, July–Dec.1992

Kipling, L., 'Punjab Cotton Prints',

Journal of Indian Art, i, no. 14, 1886

—— 'The Industries of the Punjab', *Journal of Indian Art*, ii, no. 24, 1888

Konieczny, M.G., *Textiles of Baluchistan*, London 1979

Lambrick, H.T., *Sind: A General Introduction*, repr. Jamshoro 1975, I

Langley, A.E., *Narrative of a Residence at the Court of Meer Ali Moorad*, London 1860, II

Linschoten, J.H. van, *Itinerario*, 2 vols., London 1884

Manrique, S., *Itinerario*, trans. by C. Luard, London 1927

Marshall, J., *Mohenjo-Daro and the Indus Civilization* [London 1931], repr. Karachi 1973

Martin, J.R., *Monograph on Tanning and Working in Leather in the Bombay Presidency*, London 1903

Masson, C., *Narrative of Various Journeys in Balochistan, Afghanistan, the Panjab and Kalat*, London 1843, IV

Murphy, V., *Vastra: The Fabric of Indian Art*, London [n.d.]

Nabholz-Kartaschoff, M.-L., *Golden Sprays and Scarlet Flowers: Traditional Indian Textiles from the Museum of Ethnography Basel, Switzerland*, Kyoto 1986

Nana, S., *Sindhi Embroideries and Blocks*, Karachi 1990

Paine, S., *Embroidered Textiles: Traditional Patterns from Five Continents*, London 1990

—— *The Afghan Amulet: Travels from the Hindu Kush to Razgrad*, London 1994

Postans, T., *Personal Observations on Sindh*, London 1843

Pottinger, H., *Travels in Beloochistan and Sinde; Accompanied by a Geographical and Historical Account of those Countries*, London 1816

Quentric, M., 'Notes sur les coutumes vestimentaires des Kalash de Pakistan', *Objets et Mondes*, xiii, pt. 2, 1973

Raikes, S.N., *Memoir on the Thurr and Parkur Districts of Sindh*, London 1856

Riazuddin, A., *A History of Handicrafts*, Islamabad 1988

Sandhu, C.S.C., *Dreams of Silk*, Coventry 1983

Siddiqui, I.A., *The Art of Dyeing with Vegetable and Mineral Colours*, Karachi 1976

Singh, C. and Ahivasi, D., *Woollen Textiles and Costumes from Bhara Kala Bhavan*, Benares 1981

Sorley, H.T., *Gazetteer of West Pakistan, the Former Province of Sind including*

Khairpur State, Lahore 1968

Sperber, B.G., 'Kalash: Dresses and Textile Techniques', *Proceedings of the Second International Hindukush Cultural Conference*, edd. E. Bashir and Israr-ud-Din, Karachi 1996

Steel, F.A., 'Phulkari Work in the Punjab', *Journal of Indian Art*, ii, no. 24, 1888

Stein, Sir M.A., *On Alexander's Track to the Indus: Personal Narrative of Explorations on the North West Frontier of India*, London 1929

Swarup, S., *The Arts and Crafts of India and Pakistan*, Bombay 1957

Thornton, E., *A Gazetteer of the Countries adjacent to India on the North-West, including Sinde, Afghanistan, Beloochistan, the Punjab and the neighbouring States*, London 1844

Varadarajan, L., *Traditions of Textile Printing in Kutch: Ajrak and Related Techniques*, Ahmedabad 1983

Walker, D.S., 'Classical Indian Rugs', *Hali*, iv, no. 3, 1982

Watt, G., *Indian Art at Delhi 1903: Being the Official Catalogue of the Delhi Exhibition, 1902–03*, Calcutta [1903]

Westphal-Hellbusch, S. and H.W. Westphal, *The Jat of Pakistan*, Berlin 1964

Wheeler, Sir Mortimer, 'The Indus Civilization', *Cambridge History of India*, supplementary volume, Cambridge 1953

Yacopino, F., *Threadlines Pakistan*, Karachi 1977

Glossary/Index